A SAIL ABOARD WALKABOUT
LOG BOOK - A

ALAN LONG

A SAIL ABOARD WALKABOUT
LOG BOOK - A

Thank you for your purchase of **A SAIL ABOARD WALKABOUT...Book A**

Again, thank you so much, I can really use the money.

Alan

admin@walkaboutproducts.com

Additional books published by the author:

CRAPS FOR LOW ROLLERS
ISBN 9781451524017

LOW ROLLERS GUIDE TO PROPOSITION BETS
ISBN 9781499775174

This book is dedicated to everyone that wants to stop living in a fantasy...want to go cruising, climb a mountain, cross country bike ride...write a book about a passion you have?...just make a plan and do it!

A very special thank you dedication to the wisdom of the talented folks that lived the experience of the situations, and gave them the inspiration, to come up with these wonderful quotes. They are what drives us to follow in their wake. Thank you!

Author unknown

My loving daughter gave me this plaque when I purchased *Walkabout*. I have carried it with me ever since. Thank you Jodi.

The pessimist complains about the wind; the optimist expects it to change; the realist adjusts the sails.-William A Ward

Table of Contents

FORWARD

Thank you for your interest in my *book*. It's a story about fulfilling a fantasy...a dream. That dream became a test...was I good enough to fulfill this fantasy of mine? At first, it seemed impossible, and then came a vision that maybe it could be possible after all.

I've always had a desire to share my story about this endeavor in a way that is meaningful, and hopefully, entertaining. I started writing this book in 2008 but got lost along the way. For a sailor, it has taken a lot of "tacking into the wind" to get here. This log is about beautiful memories I have that I can re-live with a smile.

I couldn't decide on the direction I wanted to take these memories *(which is why it took eleven years)* that would be the most fulfilling. 'How To' books are all over the place, and boating is just like fishing or whatever, no matter what you think you know...someone else knows more and better...and it's true, they do! Maybe make it a novel? No, I'm not that good at making things up. I decided to make it an adventure type of autobiography story/novel with some sex thrown in because everyone told me 'sex sells'...the feelings and emotions were real...not made up, and that's even better. Whew...glad to have made a decision.

It was fun to think back on the entire experience and remember the details of the hows and whys. Everything written here actually happened. I changed some of the names of the original cast and crew out of respect, and to protect myself from injury, but, they are real and very special people. The conversations I included are to paint a picture of their distinct personalities, and taken from the ships log as well as my personal log.

Why did I do it?...simply, to see if I could!

Alan

REFLECTION

1

Stuart Florida. May 1991.

Since moving aboard *Walkabout,* I am truly amazed at how beautiful the mornings are. The adventure has begun...

Fort Lauderdale, Florida. June 1996;

I spent the evening just relaxing and allowing my mind to go back in time to the first moment I laid eyes on *Walkabout*. Playing one of my many Jimmy Buffett tapes that I had acquired over the years, I could recall all of the apprehensive yet positive feelings I had that day in '91.

Everywhere I looked, I could see the projects of love that I did over the years to make *Walkabout* mine...an extension of my personality. Remembering those moments is a rewarding way to spend my last few days aboard her.

As usual, I woke up before the sun with the evocative marine aromas and feeling the gentle movement of *Walkabout*. I always loved the distinctive smell of a boat. If you have ever owned or even been aboard a boat, you know what I am talking about. It smelled like a boat, and *Walkabout* sure enough was. Many of the boats I have been aboard smelled damp and moldy and repugnant to a certain extent. Not *Walkabout*! She smelled of the ocean, varnish, teak, fiberglass and a slight hint of diesel fuel. Add those aromas to some freshly brewed coffee, and for me it was heaven.

As with any one of a thousand early mornings, I poured a cup of black coffee and made my way up the companionway and into the center cockpit...my living room. The comfort of a new day aboard was elevated by watching the golden glow of the morning sun starting at the top of the 50-foot palm trees along Las Olas Blvd., and slowly working its way down the trees as the sun rose. It is always a thrill to watch and feel the world awaken and come to colorful life. It didn't seem to matter what anchorage or marina I was in, or mountain I was on.

I always thought of *Walkabout* as more of a yacht, a fine sailing yacht. Over the years, I have come to know her every movement and what each tug or change of movement meant.....kind of a "bonding" thing.

There are some very good reasons why so many boats are named after women. It's kind of like snuggling up with your lover, and she snuggles back in the soft way that only women can. The slight tug of the dock lines as she reaches her limit in the gentle breezes giving assurance that all is well and you are still secure at the docks or at anchor. If she doesn't snuggle you back, you know you are in trouble.

You have to know her in a way that what she tells you by her movements is that you are in heaven or will soon be going to hell if you don't listen. She will never tell you in words, so pay attention to her movement.

I have come to know what each incitation has meant. If there is a change in her movement, there is going to be some kind of an event. If you weren't expecting this change or event then more than likely it is going to be bad, and you're sure going to want to find out what this "bad' is going to be. "I didn't know the anchor was dragging" is an excuse for hitting the beach, not a reason.

You never really own a boat...she owns you. I swear *Walkabout* knew there was change coming....possibly today. We had been thru quite a few adventures over the years, and I almost knew what she was going to say even before she said it. I have logged a good many miles on her hull, so we were more like very close friends.

Her potential new owners would be coming aboard soon and everything needed to be in ship shape. I had always kept her in what I called "Pristine Condition" anyway.

Some things were different today. Some personal items were removed and no longer in their proper places. Since I have never liked clutter, I installed several storage lockers and identified several hidden locations to ensure there was a place for everything. I had always been proud of *Walkabout* and never ashamed to have guest aboard at any time.

But still, all of the brightwork had an extra shine, and the varnish had just been redone. All of the spare dock lines had been washed, neatly coiled and stowed. Anything that could have been considered as clutter was removed and stowed ashore.

Oh sure, there was the fresh coffee and a Jimmy Buffett tape in the player rolling out some excellent island type of music. Those things were the same as almost any typical morning aboard *Walkabout*.

"Ahoy *Walkabout*," came the call from my friend and fellow sailor Dave. "Is this the day?" Most true boaters arise early.

"We'll see! They don't speak English, and I don't speak Italian. If nothing else it should be fun."

Dave and his sailing companion Patty, live aboard 'My Gal', a 34ft sloop docked a few slips down from *Walkabout*.

Dave, with his slender six-foot frame and blonde hair and shy demeanor, has been sailing around Florida and the Keys for several years. When I first started docking on Fort Lauderdale's Admirals Court on Hendricks Isle, Dave was living alone and berthed in the last slip at the time I arrived at the small resort. He was known as very quiet and didn't really associate with anyone and hardly ever spoke.

Dave and I had become close friends over the years, and fondly enjoyed our early morning banter. He had become an enjoyable addition to our dockside group. "Good luck," he said as he jumped on his bicycle and peddled off to work. I'm sure I will see him at the pool after work for a beer or two. Dave would take construction jobs if he was going to be in one place very long.

I had tried several other marinas during the summers refitting *Walkabout* in the "Yachting Capital Of The World" but found Admiral's Court to be the best suited for my needs. It had good access to the Inter-coastal waterway for the many trips out to the ocean, close to downtown Fort Lauderdale restaurants and shops, and boaters were allowed to work on their boats.

As with most marinas, the boaters docking here were quite a diverse group. Many of them were here when I came, and we had become a family since there were only about a dozen or so slips.

My first time at Admiral's Court was one of those special points in time that everything just seemed to click. It was like the year that your school had the unstoppable football team and there was never before or after a better class than that of '63, or the summers that you enjoyed the close group of friends and was never to be repeated. You knew that it was a very special moment in time. Life was good.

Waking up that morning just felt like I was home.

Twenty years from now you will be more disappointed by the things that you didn't do than by the ones you did do. So throw off the bowlines. Sail away from the safe harbor. Catch the trade winds in your sails. Explore. Dream. Discover.- Mark Twain

Did I mention that if the potential new owners actually do purchase *Walkabout,* they asked me if I would consider being her Captain for them to her new home in Cuba? Wait!....what?

A SAIL ABOARD WALKABOUT

DESTINY-THE BEGINNING
2

Denver, CO. Early Summer 1990.

Anchored in a small bay on Chatfield Lake on the south side of Denver aboard my 22ft. Catalina sloop Destiny.

I had power ski boats when I was younger but had always envied the sail-boaters. Sailboats are quiet and required a certain amount of skill to go from point A to point B. At this juncture in my life, if I still felt the need for speed, I had a really fast '66 Corvette roadster.

When the opportunity came up to purchase a reasonably sized sailboat in Colorado, I jumped at the chance. She was only 22 feet, had a small pop top cabin with a V-birth forward, small galley with sink and stove, table, port-a-potty, and small outboard for auxiliary power.

Also, Destiny had a full fixed keel. I liked the full keel for reasons of stability, and I considered it more of a "real" sailboat...I should have put more thought into that decision. In retrospect, a swing keel would have been better for the lake sailing I would be doing.

Swing keels are one hell of a lot easier to trailer and can be taken to shore instead of swimming or to have a dingy, which I did.

She had everything I needed to get the feel of a larger yacht. In short, I loved my little mini-yacht.

Destiny! That's the name Kathy, my first mate,

suggested would be the perfect name for my boat due to my vision of going sailing, on a "walkabout" as it were. I loved the Dundee movies.

We just finished "stepping the mast" on Destiny at Glendo Lake, Wyoming. Note the full keel.

ANCHORING OUT
AT THE LAKE
3

We are anchored in a little bay and spent last night chatting in the cockpit while enjoying a beautiful Colorado sunset with our wine, and a little romancing. Later in the evening in the V-berth with an open deck hatch, the star-filled Colorado sky shining in.

I had already brewed the morning coffee and waited in the cockpit of Destiny to watch the show. Enya was playing in the tape-deck, always a wonderfully soothing sound in the early mornings.

The sounds of rushing hot air interrupted the silence on this early morning as the balloonist were filling their balloons and preparing for take off from the south shore of Chatfield Lake. It happened almost every weekend in the summer, and it was a sight to see, anywhere from 6 to 12 beautifully colored hot air balloons filling the sky over the lake. It is just another glorious morning in Colorado with beautiful blue skies and the snow-capped Rockies as a backdrop.

As with most of my days sailing around this lake, I would close my eyes and fantasize that I was on an ocean, any ocean. Of course, Destiny would have to be a bit larger, say perhaps 40ft., and a center cockpit would be nice with a catch rig….like a vision.

"Good morning Skipper," Kathy said in her sexy sleepy morning voice. She was in the small galley pouring herself a cup of morning wake up. God, I love that term 'Skipper,' less formal than Captain but still shows a little respect.

Kathy is 5' 7" and about 125 lbs., slender with long shapely legs. She has long blonde hair, flat stomach, small chest, and a killer smile. I'm not making this up. Since Colorado mornings are very cool, especially on the water, Kathy had on a sweatshirt and sweat pants with nothing underneath.

The first time I saw Kathy, I knew I had to figure out a way to meet her. I managed to run into her again and mentioned that I had just purchased a sailboat, and that caught her interest. Better yet…we both have horses and like to ride. She oozed with a kind of cocky self-confidence that I find attractive.

"What exotic faraway island are we anchored off

of this morning, Skipper?" as she emerged from below deck.

"I was hoping you could tell me since you are the navigator," I said. "I just drive where ever you tell me to go."

We both laughed.

"Lost again are we?"

"Nope," I replied, "we are just exploring new places...never lost."

> Not all who wander are lost.
> - JR Tolkien

I loved the way she always fed my dreams. Did I mention she has a great sense of humor?

Destiny alongside the dock at Chatfield Marina

"Ya know Kathy, I have been thinking about selling my business and buying a bigger boat and cruising in the Caribbean for a few years, like, you know, go on 'walkabout.' Would you be interested?"

There was a long moment of silence as you can imagine...but, she is actually thinking about it.

"Are you serious there, Skipper?" Kathy said with flashing eyes and a big grin, "Of course! But how could we possibly do it? How much would it cost?

What would we do with our critters? (horses, cats, and dogs) What would we do with our homes? What about my job?"

Honestly, how do they come up with such questions?

We both enjoyed sailing and just being on the water. We loved new adventures and the challenges that go with them. We are horse people and have enjoyed taking our horses into the mountains for several days of camping and not seeing people for days on end, so the solitude of a long sail shouldn't be a problem.

One of the most important things when choosing a sailing companion is compatibility. It doesn't matter how good a sailor they are if you are days or weeks away from shore and then find out you don't get along. (Hmmm, it's a big ocean, and they would never find her. 'Honest, she just fell overboard in the dark!')

"We can get all of that worked out. We just need to start making a plan if you are interested." I replied. "Give it some serious thought, it would be a 'once in a lifetime' opportunity for us both."

Sipping on our morning coffee, I was thinking about how to get her back in bed, but she was thinking about other things. "Well...first, I would need to know what ocean sailing experience you have. Have you ever sailed on the ocean?" she asked. Women are so damned logical sometimes.

"You're darn right I have," I responded while interrupting my thoughts about crawling back in the V-berth.

"Back in 1978 five other IBM salesman and I

bare-boat chartered a 36 footer and sailed around the British Virgins for a week, no problems at all--so there smarty."

I didn't bother to tell her that we were so drunk most of the time, I didn't have any idea who was driving the boat or remember much about handling the rigging. I have pictures to prove that we did have a great deal of fun, however.

THE OCEAN
4

I worked in sales for IBM, one of the greatest company's in the world at the time, until 1981. A group of us decided to charter a sailboat in the British Virgin Islands and try our hand at sailing.

We were a very diverse group, to say the least. Five relative successful sales types and one successful marketing manager. Can't really say what it was that made this group work.

Banks: My best friend in the crew. Banks was an over-aged hippy from Delaware. He was just cool. Nothing ever caused the guy to lose his cool...kind of an early Fonzy type. He was the only one of us to have sailed before, so we got us a really cool Captain.

Gary: Gary and I started in sales at the same time and remained friends. A really good guy.

Neil: Neil was the manager for some of us in the group, and it never went to his head. He was a lot like us...go figure. Fantastic to be around.

John: Older than the rest of us and a perfect example of a top-notch representative for IBM. Tall, handsome guy and very smart. (not sure why he would hang with us).

Harmon: Not sure what to say about Harmon. Maybe because he was such an oddball, he just seemed to fit in and made things fun.

Alan (me): Just strange and very fortunate to know these people.

Banks had sailed on a friends boat once, and I

had an 18ft ski runabout at the time so we were no strangers to water, old salts you might say.

"One important lesson I learned while sailing in the Virgins was never take a leak off the bow while under sail or at anchor for that matter." I felt it was important to relate that bit of knowledge to Kathy's grinning face.

I took this opportunity to relate a cute survival story also. "We were out of food by the next to last day except for a can of sardines, a few crackers and one egg---my egg. Harman, one of our motley crew, had threatened to eat my egg when we returned from a night of heavy drinking ashore. I told him, in no uncertain terms, if he touched my egg he would be fish bait...I had to set up most of the night to protect my egg from my buddy Harman.

We had spent our last evening of the sail anchored off a small island beach that didn't have a dock, so we all took the dinghy ashore for the evening. The small bar on that side of the island fired up the 'ol generator for lights and to power the jukebox and speakers in the corner band area in case anyone was brave enough to sing or play the steel drums. No talent required as it turns out.

Most of our crew had taken the dinghy back out to the boat by closing time, so those of us that remained had to swim. I must say that I was a little more than apprehensive, scared actually, about swimming out to the boat after dark but too drunk and tired to care much.

The next morning I cooked the best egg I ever had in my life! Yes, Harman, it was that good! To this day, it was the best egg ever brother. But that's another story.

Me in the foreground, and Harman

"That's it? What the hell does a week in 1978 have to do with sailing on the ocean in 1991?" she inquired with a bit of skeptical curiosity.

"Well, they elected me the Captain, and then I had to tell everyone what to do and, well, you know how I hate to brag. Besides that, we went with six guys and came back with six guys. How hard can it be?"

I hope she never meets any of those guys. Besides, for all I can remember, it could have happened that way.

"And, if that's not enough I want you to know I have read Chapman's Official Sailing Guide cover to cover."

While I am on this subject of withholding some of the truthful facts from Kathy, let me point out that I don't think some women really want the whole truth sometimes. Example--"Does this dress make my butt look big? How does my special asparagus dinner taste? Wouldn't this lamp look wonderful in the living room?"

Sometimes it's just best to tell them what they want to hear. I know she really wants to go, and I am convinced that my sensitivity to her needs is one reason we get along so well.

To get away from questions about my ocean sailing experience, or lack thereof, I said, "Just give it some thought. We will have to handle any problems one at a time. The yacht club race will be starting shortly, and we need to get ready."

To get her mind on a more positive note, I pointed out that I have subscribed to Cruising World for the last five years and have read a lot about island cruising. Again, how hard can it be?

A DAY AT THE RACES
5

The Chatfield Sail & Yacht Club held races twice a week, and we were regular participants. Now, I want you to understand that I love boaters and the boating lifestyle, but some of these guys take this racing stuff very seriously, I don't, I race for fun and sun.

Many racers strip their boats to the bone for the races. I'll swear some of them even put on those goofy caps like the swimmers wear to cut down on the drag.

My idea of getting race ready was to make sure we had plenty of snacks, ice, soda, and beer. I think we were the only ones that left our cocktail table up during the races. I am sure that's why we lost so many races, but we had a great time losing.

Just another side note here...when barking out commands to the crew, it is better to label them as suggestions and not as commands or orders...I don't think the middle finger is an official boating signal...it seems some female crew-members don't take kindly to being "ordered" and offer that gesture freely!

My friend Larry "port tacking the fleet" at the start of a race

"The right of way goes to the vessel with the least competent crew"- Mike Baiocchi

In reality, Larry and his first mate Deana, are some of the most competent and experienced open water sailors on the lake. This was just bad luck crossing the start line before the horn and trying to get back in time before the start. They taught us a lot about sailing. First rule...you must be on a starboard tack and can't cross the start line until the horn.

"OK, so we are a little behind!
I like to keep an eye on the competition."

Some weather is moving in during a race.

Dropping sail after a race.

Turns out a beautiful day!

Another great Colorado sunset.

As usual, we didn't win, but we had fun, and the excitement of possibly going cruising added to the thrill of today's racing.

We continued to sail until dark and just for practice sailed into our slip without using the outboard. I always had it started just in case things went south. We had started practicing sailing out of and into our slip using the sail only, and I have to say we had gotten pretty darn good at it.

Sometimes the quarters were pretty tight, so it was always a challenge. Our arrival would generate a lot of interesting looks and fear on the faces of the other slip holders, especially the "stink potters" (power boaters).

Since I have kept a slip at Chatfield for the last several years, it was easy to make Destiny ready to sail on very short notice.

Destiny had a full keel, so she was not easy to

trailer very far, we did manage to go sailing at Glendo Lake in Wyoming and Lake Mead in Nevada.

To us, they were just different oceans. We did tend to pretend quite a bit.

The following year on the last day of the racing season, the yacht club would host a lobster dinner and trophy ceremony. Kathy and I announced that we had purchased a larger boat and would be cruising on some "big water" next season and wouldn't be back..."no, no, say it ain't so" someone yelled out, "that means someone else will have to come in last!!" Funny guy but it was true.

PRACTICE AND MORE PRACTICE

6

At the helm of Destiny.

For the rest of the summer, we used our sailing time on Chatfield for talking about going cruising and honing our sailing skills.

> *Word of caution here—when practicing a man overboard procedure make sure the person at the helm actually wants you back on-board!*

I have already mentioned how sensitive I am to Kathy's feelings but in a moment of weakness at some point a while back I might have said something to the effect that "an untrained monkey could handle a boat better than you." I was just trying to encourage her to become more proficient at the helm. Of course, I was just kidding, but it seems some women never forget—they get even.

So, with that said, always wear your personal flotation device and throw out a 50-foot recovery line before practicing your man overboard recovery procedures.

It takes some of the fun out of your day when you are trying to come up with enough words to say you're sorry while the boat circles you and you are treading water. All the while she was telling me, "get a trained monkey for crew next time....a well-trained monkey wouldn't fall overboard."

Honestly, she almost killed me!

"A small craft in an ocean is, or should be, a benevolent dictatorship." - Tristan Jones

Sailing on lakes in the western states gives a crew lots of sail change and sail handling experience. The winds are continually shifting, and you can get storms that will blow up with very short notice.

This practice did prove very useful in the coming years. We were always looking for the best ways to handle any weather change situation. Lots of trial and error proved to be the best way to learn from experiences. Again, caution...some mistakes you can only make once.

By nature, I tend to be a very cautious sailor. Every trip out onto the lake we would practice reefing the main and dropping the jib. We have never been "knocked down" by a strong wind, but I have seen it happen...it does not appeal to me, so recovering from a knockdown is not something I plan on practicing.

Avoidance is best on this one, especially on a larger boat.

SEE UNDER THE SEA
7

Over the summer our plans were proceeding toward our goal of ocean sailing next year, so we decided we should take scuba lessons. Not only because of the opportunity to see some beautiful reefs and fish, I know there would be a need to do work on the hull of the boat from time to time.

We were recommended to take lessons at Rocky Mountain Dive Center in Lakewood, CO. which we did.

Being the type of people Kathy and I are we quickly became friends with Tom, the manager, and our instructor, he was especially interested in our plans to go sailing. Tom allowed us to use the pool and equipment at the dive center at any time we wanted more pool time. He was always available to answer any questions we had, and I felt we were getting some special attention.

Me being underwater has to be a lot like a fish being out of the water, and I am told I look just about as graceful, but I just learned to cope. I think part of Tom's special interest in us was because he didn't want to have a student drown in his pool.

Also, it's not easy to laugh underwater.

Our "guppy" scuba class.

The scuba lessons were some of the most fun you can have underwater only to be outdone by actually diving on a coral reef in the Florida Keys, which is the first place we will head after we are certified.

For the most part, our lessons were pretty uneventful. We did learn the valuable buddy system of diving and that you don't fool around underwater. People can die under there.

Our open water dives were at Chatfield Lake, and the visibility was all of twelve inches, we called them braille dives. It was a lot like night diving except when you turn on your dive light you still can't see anything. We kept track of our buddy mostly by feel which can be fun, and you have to keep your mind on which way is up since you can't see the bubbles. Up is very important.

If you aren't familiar with diving, one essential piece of gear is called a buoyancy compensator device, or BC for short. A BC, or BCD as they are called, has several valuable uses and one of which is to adjust your buoyancy to neutral so you can stay at a given depth without sinking or floating to the surface and as a result allowing the diver to swim and enjoy the scenery without fighting to stay at a certain depth. This is accomplished by adding or decreasing the air in the BC. A good BC can not only save your life but makes the entire experience more pleasurable.

So, if you can't see your bubbles, and you are in a poor visibility environment, you won't know which way to swim. Got it? If you add some air, however, you will start up. You just don't want to go up too fast.

Divers can become disoriented and confused due to many other factors, so safety is the first priority.

You might laugh but remember we wear weights to sink us and at some point, you will want to quit sinking, so the BC is one of your best friends.

Much of this type of experience has added to the teamwork required for sailing. You dive using the buddy system, and you need to know your buddies moves and that you can count on them. You should sail as a team and dive as a team.

We were ready for our first dive trip, so plans were made to head to Florida for some great diving and boat shopping. Life is good.

A SAIL ABOARD WALKABOUT

BOAT SHOPPING IN PARADISE

8

It was starting to get cold in Denver that early fall morning as we boarded the plane for Miami. The sun had not yet appeared on the horizon, but it was going to be another glorious Colorado day by the look of the eastern sky.

I wanted to get into Florida early enough to look at some boats in the Miami area first. We had a full schedule set up to look at boats and to try out our newly acquired diving skills as well in the Florida Keys.

"Are you allowing any time for eating and sleeping?" my dive buddy asked. Sometimes women can be so sarcastic.

"Yeess! Around midnight sounds great, swab."

I had been in contact with Florida Yacht Sales and a representative by the name of Robert. Robert is a sailor himself. Over the course of our conversations, I had told him what I was looking for and see if he could arrange for us to look at some boats that I might be interested in during our trip.

Based on my dreams, and articles that I had read, I told him I was looking for something in the 36 to 45 foot range, center cockpit, ketch rig, well equipped and in Bristol Condition, (In boating terms Bristol means pristine or the best condition) oh, and by-the-way, under $50,000 and white and blue would be nice.

Robert swears to this day that we were cut off because of the Bermuda Triangle thing and that he didn't hang up on me.

We had become friends during our many phone calls, and I am sure he wouldn't lie to me.

I had been to South Florida several times when I was with IBM and really enjoyed the diversity of this city, but this was Kathy's first time, and we both fell in love with it from the moment we got off the plane.

Robert had arranged three yacht showing for this afternoon, and we were to meet him at their offices on South Miami Beach not far from Joe's Stone Crab, one of my favorite places to eat.

"Wow! We are really here, in Florida, and going to look at some boats. I can't believe it!" I said.

My excitement grew as we drove across the MacArthur Causeway toward Miami Beach. I could see the masts of the boats in the large marina on the south end of the island. I loved the sight, sound, and smell of the ocean at the marina, diesel and all. A large cruise ship was just leaving the port as we crossed the causeway.

After lunch at Joe's, we met with Robert to start our boat shopping adventure. He had set up three showings but had already informed me that none of them met my criteria. Oh...OK.

It seems price might be a problem also. Go figure. He could fix me up with everything I was looking for, but the prices would be around $50,000 **more** than I was looking to spend. I could go with a smaller boat in the 30-35 foot range sloop-rigged or a fixer-upper. The latter didn't appeal to me because I wanted to get started without a long dock time "fixing things up." I fully expect to do some work, but I don't want to rebuild the entire boat. I really wasn't interested in anything older than ten years either.

Robert did show me the ranges of what I could expect, and that gave me an idea of what I could get for my money. It was a good start, and I now know I would need to change my expectations. In no way did this dampen my excitement. Just being on the boats did indeed increase my enthusiasm.

I couldn't help but wonder where these boats had been and the adventures that their crews had experienced.

Robert also pointed out the extreme lack of center cockpit ketch rigged boats for sale since most sailors preferred the more traditional sloops with aft cockpits.

Robert did find some blue and white boats to look at.

Just what I was looking for only larger and way more expensive.

Finally, a boat I can afford! Well, OK, I can add some white paint. Not quite a center cockpit however...more like a full cockpit.

KEY LARGO
THE CONCH REPUBLIC
9

Early the next morning, armed with our new insight into the world of sailing yachts, we headed south to the Florida Keys and our destination in the town of Marathon on Vaca Key.

It was an almost magical trip heading south on the fabled Highway 1 into the keys. The skies were clear and almost a royal blue hue, contrasting with the beautiful shoal draft blue water of the Atlantic on the left and the Gulf of Mexico on the right. I felt like I was coming home even though I had never been this far south.

I was surprised, and a little disappointed, to learn that coconut palm trees were not native to Florida or the Caribbean for that matter. The Keys were mostly covered with various types of mangrove and palmetto as well as royal palm trees. I had visions of climbing a coconut tree and having some fresh coconut milk with my first mate.

Kathy and I talked about the boats we had seen and the knowledge Robert had shared with us about what to look for in our shopping. Also, what type of equipment and gear we would need, and the approximate costs that would be incurred, if the boat didn't already have them. I had quickly become aware that I really didn't have a clue what was involved in ocean sailing or island cruising for that matter.

With all of the boat talk and daydreaming the time flew by faster than first-grade recess, and we found ourselves looking at a WELCOME TO KEY LARGO sign. The first thought that came into my mind was that of Humphrey Bogart, why I'm not sure, I should have thought more about Lauren Bacall instead. Then the sign that read, WELCOME TO THE CARIBBEAN CLUB WHERE THE WORLD-FAMOUS MOVIE KEY LARGO WAS FILMED.

One of our favorite songs at the time was Kokomo by The Beach Boys.....go ahead and try to get that song out of your mind now.

I started thinking about a little *afternoon delight, cocktails and you at night...we* never had much trouble in that respect anyway.

This place will have to be a definite stop on our next trip to the Keys, and I was sure there would be many more trips. *(As a matter of fact, a pretty significant event would take place for us here in a few years.)*

MARATHON, FLORIDA
10

The drive down the Florida Keys to Marathon was very pleasurable, especially with our lapses in and out of reality. We located our "hotel" with very little trouble.

The accommodations were fittingly nautical in nature. Our "hotel" was actually a houseboat docked in Boot Key Harbor. They were like floating condominiums, including full kitchens and far exceeded our expectations. Things just kept getting better....!

After checking into our floating hotel room, we ventured out to explore Marathon and become a little more familiar with local folklore and about life in the Keys. I felt a need to somehow fit in and not stand out as a 'tourist,' so we had to get some local color. Of course one of the best ways to gain local color is to visit local bars, so that's what we did. I know it's a tough job, but it just had to be done.

The local watering hole we chose was just as we imagined it would be – a little on the dark side as far as lighting is concerned, overlooking the Florida Bay, a dark wooden bar with some tarnished brass trimmings and several mounted fish and pictures of proud fisherman with their catches. It had that smell of an oceanfront bar that I grew to love so much. Definitely not a Chart House.

We sat at the bar close to a fellow that had the appearance of a seafaring man that introduced himself as "Pots." No, this wasn't a local connection for anything. Pots explained his nickname comes from his profession of having lobster traps, commonly called lobster pots, in a certain area on the Atlantic side of the Keys. Just the drinking companion we had hoped to find.

Pots was kinda on the big side but not fat, more muscled than anything, and appears not to have shaved for several days. He wore a well-used Captain's hat and a not exactly clean white T-shirt. I thought for sure he would pull out a pipe and lite it, kinda like Popeye. Pots has lived in various location in the Keys for over twenty years after moving from the Boston area and settled in Marathon because of the quality and quantity of lobsters.

Since Kathy and I both loved lobster, we were fascinated by this lobster trap thing. Pots went on to explain the traps, called pots by many locals, were designed so that once a lobster entered the pot for the bait, he could not escape, something to do with lobsters can't swim backward.

The best locations are near reefs with a sandy bottom, and the pots are weighted down and have a line secured to a buoy floating on the surface to identify their location.

Pots was not very fond of pleasure boaters. It seems that these buoy lines of his have a tendency to get wrapped up in propellers and caught on sailboat rudders and keels. Not only does the pot fisherman lose some of their equipment they also would lose the catch that may be in the pot due to the fact they can't find the pot on the bottom or the entire setup may even be stolen.

Kathy asked, "Couldn't people just dive down and take the lobster or just pull the pot up by the line and have a lobster dinner?"

This question seemed to bring up some bad feelings from Pots, and he proceeded to let us know, "people can get seriously hurt if they are caught stealing lobster pots. Lobster-men can be pretty short-tempered about those things." I could tell Pots wasn't kidding.

Little did we know we would have some experience with these things in later years. I always wondered if any of them belonged to Pots.

We enjoyed spending our first afternoon listening to stories of fishing and the sea with several other boatmen at the bar joining in on our "teach the cow-folks from Colorado a thing or two about island life" conversation.

We learned the town name of Marathon dates back to the late 1800s and early 1900"s when the Florida East Coast Railroad was being built by some fancy pants New Yorker by the name of Henry Flagler. The idea was to build a railroad all the way to Key West. The railroad workers were working night and day to complete the railway, and many of the workers complained that "this is getting to be a real Marathon," the name stuck and was used to name the local railroad station.

The town of Marathon is actually located on several Keys, Knight's Key, Boot Key, Vaca Key, Fat Deer Key, Long Point Key, Crawl Key, and Grassy Key and is located in the middle of the Florida Keys chain.

Today, many of the bridges connecting the Keys were once railroad bridges that have been converted for automobiles.

One of the more colorful items that Pots and the gang were most proud of is the time the Florida Keys seceded from the Union (United States) in 1982 and became The Conch Republic. Seriously now...this is really cool!

Ya know what!? Pots really did pull out his pipe and lite it as he proceeded to tell us about the Conch Republic.

It seems the U.S. Border Patrol set up a blockade on U.S. Highway 1 at Florida City and Keys residence had to prove their citizenship in order to leave the Keys and drive to the mainland. This act irritated the Mayor of Key West (Dennis Wardlow), so much that he announced that the Conch Republic not only seceded from the Union but also declared war on the United States by hitting a man dressed in a U.S. Navy uniform over the head with a stale loaf of Cuban bread and then surrendered to the Admiral in charge of the Navy base in Key West after a one minute war.

Just when I didn't think this story could get any funnier Pots said the Conch Republic then demanded 1 Billion dollars in foreign aid to rebuild after the war. I gotta tell ya we were all laughing so hard it hurt...the entire bar was going crazy.

Reluctantly, after several hours, we had to leave our new friends and bid them farewell. The bar had started to fill up with both the locals as well as tourist and we began to get the feeling of being "old salts" by this time. Besides, my gut was still hurting not only from laughing but from hunger as well.

A tourist remains an outsider throughout his visit, but a sailor is part of the local scene from the moment he arrives. - Anne Davision

Hall's Dive Adventures used Faro Blanco Marina & Resort to dock their boats, so we decided to have dinner in at a restaurant located near the marina and explore the local boating life.

I just can't get enough of the marinas. Here we go with the smells and sounds of marina life, salt water, fish, diesel fuel, halyards clanking, birds squawking in delight. Some of the fishing boats had come in with their fresh catches, and I gotta tell ya the birds were going crazy. What a sight to see for us landlubbers.

Faro Blanco is located on the gulf side of the Key, and the sunset was more spectacular than we could have expected. We spent most of the early evening enjoying the sights and sounds of this busy marina and pretending we were part of it, and discussing what we learned about the Conch Republic and lobster traps.

It turned out to be a very romantic evening, and we couldn't wait to get back to our floating hotel room.

When we returned to our floating condo, something was not right. I know we had more than a few drinks but...WOW..., when we left the unit I remember we walked down a ramp to get to the dock. Now, we had to walk down the ramp again to get to our unit.

"This just ain't right," I said to the now bewildered Kathy.

We both kind of shrugged, and Kathy said, "Let's worry about it in the morning."

After relating the story to our dive instructor, I was suitably embarrassed, I just gotta learn more about this whole tide thing.

FIRST DAY DIVING
11

Being as excited as kids on Christmas morning, we were up with the sun and looking forward to our first full day in the Keys.

It was as beautiful sunrise as you can imagine with the first glow of light outlining the boats anchored in Boot Key Harbor along with the gentle lapping of the waves from a passing boat on our floating hotel room, and there were all the birds gliding over the water looking for their breakfast.

Did I pass away during the night and sail right on up to Heaven? After such a passion filled romantic evening, I couldn't imagine a better way to go.

My friend Tom at Rocky Mtn. Dive suggested we book our dives with Hall's Dive Adventures for our first dives and since ya gotta trust your dive instructor that's who we chose. They rent first-rate equipment, since we didn't have our own yet, and offer a variety of dive trips based on our level of experience, and what we want to see under the sea.

We arrived early to get a feel for what the day would bring and give ourselves some time for our nerves to settle down a bit.

Several people would be diving with us, so this extra time gave us a chance to meet some of them and get a start on becoming shipmates.

I felt a need to make friends with some of my fellow shipmates just in case I got into trouble under the sea and needed help. I sure didn't want to give Kathy an opportunity to "teach me a lesson," remember the "man overboard drills" I talked about earlier at the lake??

Our check-in and equipment checkouts went smoother than I expected, thanks to the staff at Hall's. They briefed us on the dives we would be taking today since they don't determine them until they know what the weather and sea conditions will be on the day of the dives.

Today is the day I really started my education of the open sea and the preparation it takes to cast off and head out of the safety of the marina. These guys were pros, and I wanted to learn everything I could from them...especially the Captain/Dive Master. After all, I was going to be a Captain someday!

The name of our dive boat was Lady Key Diver, and the Skippers name was Jack. Now, I really liked Jack as Captain/Dive Master, but when he started hitting on Kathy I was pretty sure I didn't like that.

Matter of fact I damn well didn't like it! Just because he was solid muscle and well tanned...Kathy said he had a nice smile. Oh, OK.

Our Captain Jack...Kathy took this picture because she wanted to get the name of the boat. It should have been centered better don't ya think?

Oh well, I was interested in his mind and knowledge.

As we headed to our first dive at Sombrero Key (reef), we started passing the floating buoy markers of what turned out to be lobster pots, and that started me thinking about our conversations with "Pots" in the bar yesterday.

Kathy was sure spending a lot of time talking to Captain Jack but I was sure she was just getting some tips about navigating on the ocean and stuff like that.

Captain Cracker-Jack was a master at maneuvering Lady Key Diver as close to the reef as allowed and in with the other dive boats. He was very informative about what we were going to see and some of the things we should watch out for...such as barracuda, eels and sharks.

Wait!!! What?? Sharks?? I hadn't thought about

them.

"Did he just say sharks?" I asked Kathy.

"He sure did Skipper," she replied with a smile. She could be so cocky at times.

Now I am hearing the theme from Jaws...da da, da da, how big did he say this boat is? Tourist are protected, right???

Kathy said Captain Jack-ass told her that "most divers never even see a shark, so there is nothing to really worry about."

Kathy is so damn fearless, and I hate snakes and sharks.

So maybe that's what she and Captain Jack-off were talking and laughing about on the ride out.

I once had an experience with a very large barracuda.....

It was in the late '70s while snorkeling in the Virgin Islands with my IBM buddies, one of those monsters decided to protect our boarding ladder from intruders. Unfortunately, we were the intruders that he kept from boarding. All six of us were in the water, and this monster barracuda was preventing us from getting out. They have very sharp teeth ya know! Some of those cuda's were over four feet long half of that length being teeth.

With nobody aboard to move the boat, we had to figure a way to get at least one of us back aboard to get away from this guy.

One of our fellow snorkelers, Banks, decided he had enough and needed to get aboard posthaste, so he started to shimming up the anchor line like Spider-man. It was an amazing thing to watch.

Once Banks started the engine, our ladder protector decided it was time to move on.

Lesson learned...don't wear anything shiny while in the water with barracuda. I think barracuda have a feminine side that is attracted to gold, silver, and diamonds. Look it up if you don't believe me.

Since I mentioned my thoughts about that to Kathy, I am sure she took it wrong.

OK, back to our dive. Our fellow divers included a couple from Minnesota and a couple of guys that were experienced divers, one of which had to weigh over 300 lbs. His name was Ken, and I couldn't imagine how he could be a diver.

You know that feeling of butterflies you get in your stomach when you are going to do something exciting? Well, underwater it's not butterflies...it's jellyfish. WOW!! Once you get over the hyperventilating and relax it is wonderful, and it's an entirely different world, and you can breathe in it.

Speaking of jellyfish, you have to watch out for them too.

There are really a lot of things in the oceans that want to eat you or, at the very least, want to hurt you or will hurt you if you go poking around them. I had a run in with a Portuguese man o' war in Hawaii in the '70s, and I want to tell you it hurt like hell for days. He stung me on my left shoulder and all the way down my arm. Look these guys up and get an idea of what the treatments are.

Now before the "everything correct" folks get involved I know the man o' war is not really a jellyfish but is a siphonophore. It looks like a jellyfish and hurts like hell if it stings you and that's all there is to it.

OK, back to our dive again. Once we got into the water, and all of the trouble getting under the water, it was simply breathtaking.

Everywhere we looked, there was the beauty of the reef. Gorgonians, brain, finger and lettuce corals can be seen everywhere along with schools of tropical fish of all shapes and colors. Glorious!

Out of the corner of my eye, I notice a large dark creature swimming nearby. I tapped Kathy on the shoulder to take a peak, it was Ken!! He was as graceful a swimmer I have ever seen. This extremely large man was moving about in the water as though he was Aqua-man himself. His dive partner was just as good, and they were a pleasure to watch. Why can't I be like that? I really am not very graceful underwater.

Ken, aka Aqua-man

Me, as graceful as a fish out of water.

It didn't take me long to get used to breathing with a more or less normal rhythm and start to relax and enjoy this "beyond imagined" first time experience.

There were so many new things to see and explore along with the beauty of the reef. I saw some movement in one hole in the reef and upon further investigation discovered that hole belongs to an eel that poked his head out and warned me to stay away....wise man that I am, I left him alone.

Oh, and by the way, we saw a shark that Captain Jack-of-all-things-in-the-ocean said very few divers ever see. That made me feel special. It turned out to be a small harmless nurse shark but a shark none the less.

The bottom time went by way too fast, and it was time to get out of our newly discovered 'under the waves' world and return to the land of homo sapiens.

Back aboard the Lady Key Diver, I had to ask Ken about his diving grace underwater. He said he had been diving for many years, and it is the only time in his waking hours that he is not in pain because of his weight. WOW...never thought of that. He is weightless in the water and therefore no pain.

Our second dive of the day was at East Washerwoman Shoal and although not as spectacular as Sombrero Key it was still great. Of course, I had to make some off-hand comment about "Washerwoman," and at some point in time I will have to pay for my wise-ass remarks.

Kathy did manage to find a large and very beautiful conch shell and, unbeknownst to me, put it in her dive bag. *I swear we were not aware that doing so was illegal!*

Overall our first real dives in the blue waters were fantastic. We both lived to tell our tales of adventure when we got back to the mountains and thanks to a Kodak plastic waterproof disposable camera, we had pictures to prove it.

The only casualty of the dives was I lost my dive

knife.

Since this was our last day in the Keys, we decided to head on down to Key West and have a relaxing dinner and experience the glorious sunset at "lands end" known as Mallory Square. We had set our watches and our attitudes to "island time" days ago and didn't want it to end.

I didn't find a boat that I really wanted or could afford on this trip, but I did manage to learn more than I thought possible about different kinds of sailboat designs with Robert's help. With my newly acquired knowledge, I can now narrow my search for my perfect mini-yacht.

The plane trip back to Denver was very reflective and quiet as we were both thinking about everything we had seen and experienced.....and smelled!?

Smelled?? "What the hell is that smell? Kathy, tell me you packed that conch shell in a checked bag right?"

"NO..."! She was so proud of her find she wanted to show it off.

The entire plane was beginning to smell like a garbage dump at high noon on a 110-degree day. It turned out the shell had been occupied, and the little critter suffered a horrible death and wanted the world to know it. The small carry-on travel bag could not contain the very repugnant odor any longer. The bag went to the trash, but the beautiful conch shell is still proudly on display. (*I think we're still not allowed to board a United flight.*)

NARROW THE SEARCH
12

*My boat needs enough room to have cocktails for
6, dinner room for 4, and bedroom for 2.*

It is time to focus in on the type of sailing we were going to be doing. Around the world or lots of blue-water sailing? No, although that would be an incredible ambition, just not a dream that could become a reality, especially at this point.

Coastal cruising? Oh for sure there would be a great deal of coastal cruising involved at least for the first year.

Armed with my new found knowledge of all types of sailboats, I now know just what kind of boat I want. I definitely want a center cockpit in the 35 to 40 feet range in length. One nice thing, for me at least, about center cockpits is that I sat higher above the water and have a better view of what's going on around my boat.

Another big reason is with a boat that big, along with uncertainty about the abilities of the crew, I could respond quicker fore and aft of the boat quicker and with greater ease. *(This proved to be very useful while single-handing sailing.)*

In addition to the above advantages of the center cockpit is the aft stateroom layouts. The aft stateroom allows for plenty of stand up headroom and greater privacy from the main salon and forward stateroom. Additionally, with a large hatch directly above the bed, I can be on deck quicker in an emergency, instead of going through the main salon and up the companionway. *(The ability to do this also proved to be very useful in the coming years.)*

You must understand that I have plans for many romantic evenings abroad my boat and that would include in some great erotic experiences.

For the sail plan, I really like the idea of a ketch rig due to the choice of sail options available to handle almost every type of weather condition. Ketch rigged boats look really cool under full sail also, and I really want to look "cool."

A few of the benefits with a split rig of a ketch:

First, they offer greater flexibility for sail reduction, with the added ability for under sail options, allowing a jib and mizzen configuration in strong winds, for example.

Secondly, at anchor with the mizzen set as a steadying sail, the boat will lay comfortably head-to-wind.

A cruising sloop of a similar size boat has only two large sails to make up the same sail area as a ketch, and can considerably more difficult for a short-handed crew to handle.

A ketch rig is not the best choice for windward sailing, but it can make an ideal cruising sailboat.

And then there is a seemly endless list of options, oh wait, make that just an "endless list" because every option has more options, and equipment that every sailboat needs, or should have. And, the list grows depending on how you intend to sail, the locations you wish to sail, and of course the money you are willing or able to spend.

An important consideration is the keel. As a matter of explanation for the beginner sailor, the keel is the bottom section of a sailboats hull and acts to counteract the sideways movement of the boat due to wind and waves and provides greater tracking thru the water. The keel also may contain ballast, a material used for weight, to provide stability and keep the boat upright and lessen the tendency to heel excessively.

Ballast can also help a sailboat sink, and that's a not a good thing.

There are dozens of types of keels available on boats these days, and all of them have advantages and disadvantages. Since I, we, are planning on most of our sailing to be along coastal waters to start with, but some open blue water sailing on occasion, I wanted to stay with a shoal draft keel with a centerboard that could be lowered in the open water.

On larger boats, a shoal draft is more or less around four feet of draft, and the centerboard would add another four feet thus giving more lateral resistance when lowered for sailing close to the wind and in open water but a shallower draft and less drag when raised for sailing downwind or in shallow water.

Other popular kinds of keels consist of Full Keel, Fin Keel, and Swing Keel. As mentioned, each has its own set of advantages and disadvantages, so decide what type of sailing you will be doing the most.

One of the boats Robert showed us was an Irwin 37ft center cockpit sloop. Irwin is not considered a top name in the boating world, but I found you can get a lot of boat for the money in the used boat market. Remember, for me, us, to do this, I am on a tight budget.

I would have to sacrifice many of the features I was looking for to buy a higher quality sailboat or give up on the entire thing...not an option for me. I'm not planning an around-the-world type of cruise. Primary use would be island hopping in the Florida Keys and the Bahamas to start, and depending on how that goes, possibly head deeper into the Caribbean.

There is so much to learn, and since I didn't

know what to expect, I felt the need to take smaller steps, and start getting a real sense of what things would be like. Like, what if I went overboard, so to speak, by buying more than was needed to start out, and then discover this wasn't going to work. It's hard to undo what's overdone.

Now my search was narrowed to that exact boat but with a ketch rig instead of a sloop.

FINALLY, I FOUND HER
13

During the past few months, I made the decision to sell the business that we had started from scratch eleven years ago...just my beautiful wife and me. Starting and operating the business cost me my marriage, but it was something I needed to do. I went thru so many mixed emotions about selling, but it was time. The business was very successful and allowed me to provide jobs (28 on the payroll) for some wonderful people...100's over the years.

The business contributed nicely to the economy of Golden, Colorado, I town that I love, and it was praised for its valuable service, but I was getting burned out. I had accomplished a primary goal that I had set for myself early in life...succeed in business(s). The business story warrants another book someday.

As I was drooling all over the pages of my latest issue of Cruising World, I found *Marigold*. That's it!! That's the boat I have been looking for right down to the blue stripe. It seemed to have everything I am looking for.

Marigold...that name would have to go. I'm a cowboy from Colorado. Columbine (state flower) would have a better chance. Having a yacht named *Marigold* is like having a horse named Flower or a dog named Fluffy. Not gonna happen!

Marigold was located in a marina in Stuart/Port Salerno/Hobie Sound area of Florida, so I called Robert to see if he could take time out of his busy schedule of NOT finding me a boat and check out MY find! "Please let me know what you think as soon as possible and send me some pictures," I said.

"Aye aye skipper," came his reply. Man, I like the sound of that.

It didn't take long for Robert to check out *Marigold* and get back to me. I think he would do anything to get rid of me at this point.

He said the price seemed fair, and that a proper survey should determine if there are any problems that weren't evident to him or the average buyer. He did point out a few minor concerns, but nothing that should be of a significant problem and the pictures were in the mail.

Robert recommended I contact a qualified marine surveyor to perform a proper survey of *Marigold* before going too far overboard. Funny guy.

I received the photos in just a few days and told Kathy, "I'm coming up the mountain tonight with a with a bottle of wine and a dozen photos of *Marigold*."

"Great! Came her reply. "I can't think of a better way to spend an evening with it starting to snow outside, you, a bottle of wine, and some pictures of your potential new yacht." I'll make sure the fire is going strong for you." That woman's a great fire starter, also handy on camping trips.

I immediately checked my schedule the next morning and looked at available flights to Florida. I had Robert check his schedule to make sure we could meet in Stuart to check it out.

I decided to throw off the lines and set sail for Miami, FL. and check out *Marigold* to see if she's worthy of a name change to *Walkabout*. *Walkabout* is the name Kathy and I decided to call our yacht if we ever got one. Perfect name. Like I mentioned before, I loved the Dundee movies and the idea of "going on walkabout" just fit both of us.

It was mid-April in Denver, and we just had one of those famous snowstorms that dumped 12 inches of snow, so I was leaving at the perfect time. Cold and snow in Denver and heading to sunny Florida to look at what I hoped would be our ambition come true.

It's all set. If I like it, I had gotten a list of surveyors and arranged for one of them to be on call if I needed him. The Martha's Vineyard owners were already in Port Salerno boat shopping themselves for a replacement for *Marigold* (they are looking at trawlers for more comfortable cruising). They had purchased *Marigold* new in '82 and used her for cruising the Bahamas every winter.

Marigold is docked at David Lowe's Boatyard and located in the Manatee Pocket in Port Salerno/Hobie Sound off the St Lucie River. Lowe's happens to be a full-service boatyard and can handle pretty much anything a boat owner would need including haul-outs that are important to do a proper survey.

A note about surveyors. Boat surveying was not regulated at that time, and there was not a governing agency. The best I could do is to look to The American Boat And Yacht Council (ABYC) since they have members that are also surveyors. Unless you really trust the owner and/or boatyard, it is best to find your own surveyor for obvious reasons.

After landing in Miami, I picked up my rental car and headed north to Port Salerno/Hobie Sound on the Florida Turnpike. I wanted to take highway A1A that pretty much follows the Inter-coastal Waterway, but it would have taken longer. I wanted to get by the boatyard before dark. I made sure my cheap motel was on A1A.

After checking in at the Motel 6, I took off for the boatyard using a map the guy at the front desk of the motel made for me. I figured I would be too late and they might be closed. I wanted to check it out so I could get an early start tomorrow. Yep, they were closed.

I could see what appeared to be a park across the water and figured I could get a better view of Lowe's marina and just maybe see *Marigold* at the docks. I took side roads around Manatee Pocket and located the park. With my binoculars, I found her. There she was, mostly identified by her ketch rigging and blue stripe. Love at first sight, I'm thinking...I know I felt a tingle.

I drove around Port Salerno and started really enjoying the smell and feel of the port. Port Salerno is a finger bay off the St. Lucie River and has what seems to me to have a very quaint charm with older homes and lots of boatyards and marinas. Very quiet. Kind of an older middle-class community. They even have an original Dairy Queen. The building looks like an ice cream cone on the top. I'm gonna get a cone tomorrow. I am comfortable here.

The next town to the north is Stuart. Stuart is

larger, with more shopping options.

As soon as I returned to the motel, I called Kathy and could barely contain my excitement. She wanted to know everything about the trip so far and couldn't believe I located *Marigold* in the almost darkness.

"I didn't think it strange at all.." I had thought she knew me better than that.

"From the distance, Marigold looked just like the photo in Cruising World," I said. "I wish you were here so we could check her out together." I miss the girl even though she backtalk's me on occasion.

I gave her my impression of Port Salerno, "I think this is the kind of place that would be fun to hang out for a while, and you would enjoy it! It really fits into the vision of my dream, our dream actually, about doing this...you know, the whole walkabout thing."

"Sounds wonderful, I can't wait to hear what you have to say about *Marigold*."

"I am going to be there first thing in the morning even though the appointment to inspect Marigold isn't until 10:00. I want to absorb as much as I can about the entire marina/boatyard environment," I told her.

ABOARD MARIGOLD
14

I arrived at David Lowe's boatyard around eight. I was impressed with the size and scope of the place. Boats of all types and sizes were spread out over the grounds. There was a crew in the process of hauling out a large sport fisher type of boat with a large boat cradle type of thing. There was a small, older fellow, driving the lift and directing all the action, and he was looking at me in a suspicious kind of way.

I decided to find the office to see if I can get permission to go onto the docks and find *Marigold*. As I entered the office, I was greeted by a middle-aged lady with a charming attitude and a business like manor named Peggy. I could tell from my IBM sales experience that this woman probably ran the place and carried a lot of weight with the boss.

I explained to Peggy what I was doing as far as buying a boat and the reason I was there. She has known the owners of *Marigold* for many years since they have wintered *Marigold* at Lowe's. But, she needs to clear it with Mr. Lowe first to get permission to go to the docks. He was hauling out a boat right now so it may be awhile.

I sorta had a hunch that the little older fella driving the lift might be the owner. Peggy called him on the radio, and he said he would come in when he finished. I enjoyed watching the rest of the haul-out and placement of the sport fisher into an open spot in the boatyard on a massive array of supports.

Mr. Lowe finished his haul-out and came into

the office, Peggy gave him a brief explanation I why I was there. Mr. Lowe was very short on conversation and said he had already spoken with the Ericsons at their boat, and I could go ahead to the docks. I informed Peggy that Robert would be showing up at 10:00. She remembered him when he came to check out the boat the first time.

I was so impressed with this older business owner working his dream. I'm sure he built this business from what was once just a thought he had once.

As I approached the slip where *Marigold* was docked the butterfly's in my stomach felt more like a flock of seagulls.

I knew as soon as I stood up close to *Marigold* that she would be mine. She has the features, layout, and rigging that I was looking for...even the correct color trim. The overall condition seemed good, as far as this cowboy is concerned. Danger, danger...in my mind I already own her. Not good before negotiations even start.

The owners, Eric and Dorthy Ericson, came up from below deck and Eric introduced himself and his wife Dotty or Dot. Since I showed up early, I got a chance to meet and chat with them before their representative arrived. They saw me drooling all over the side of *Marigold*.

They were from Block Island, R.I. Block Island is about 14 miles south of Long Island, N.Y. and 13 miles south of R.I. and is considered a coastal archipelago. They told me, "It's reported that the famous pirate William Kidd visited and stayed awhile around 1700 and enriched a few locals."

What a pleasure it is to meet these real sailors. These are the kind of people that I have read about and envy. I enjoy Listening to some of the adventures that they shared on *Marigold* over the years and their plans for coming years. *Marigold* has meant a lot to them, and their pride showed.

How cool is this? Kind of like meeting your football hero or an astronaut or someone!

Eric asked if I would like to come aboard and tour the *Marigold* even though it was early and his representative hadn't arrived yet, and neither had mine, "Yes, I would really like to do that" I tried to mask my excitement.

Eric gave me a tour of the main deck, and the different types of gear *Marigold* is equipped with.

A partial list of the gear that is included and is an excellent start to what I consider, at this point anyway, a minimally equipped boat that could sail the inter-coastal or some moderate off-shore cruising. She is basically ready to go. Even an almost full tank of diesel.

- Masts and booms had been replaced three years ago with all new fittings.
- Four sails including the main, mizzen, 130% roller furling genoa (jib), and beautiful spinnaker.
- Bowsprit with anchor roller.
- 12-volt electric windlass with 250 ft of rode and chain and two anchors.
- VHF marine radio.
- Raytheon 12 mile radar.
- Apelco Loran.
- Auto Helm 6000 and Tiller Master.
- Life Sling w/Rescue Ring, Pole and Light.
- EPIRB (Emergency Position Beacon)

- Perkins Spare Parts Engine Kit.
- Speed, Depth, and Wind Indicator.

Fire extinguishers and life vests were also included of course along with dozens of other small items that are needed.

The tender (dingy/inflatable) was not included in the price he is asking, so I looked at that as a possible bargaining item.

Dingy, inflatable, tender, or "life-raft." No matter what it is called or style of boat it is, it's essential to have one on the onboard. Deciding what kind to have depends on the type of cruising you are going to be doing...at least at the start. Like everything else, everyone has an opinion. They all have their good and bad points. Decide what's best for you and your crew to start with.

Eric pointed out that they used theirs to explore many small islands without having to move Marigold. Having an outboard made exploring so much easier than rowing, which they would not do. It's a poor excuse for a true "life-raft," but it's better than swimming.

For the truly uneducated, like me, all the lines, and both standing and running rigging appeared to be in great shape.

The center cockpit..ah, yes...I could imagine that the center cockpit would become my floating man cave. Eric and I had the same reasons for liking its location, being almost in the center of the boat. The cockpit also has a full dodger, Bimini top, and side-curtains for foul weather as well as a complete set of screens. There seemed to be almost enough room to ride a bike around the deck. (which we actually did in the islands).

I'm not real good at hiding my feelings, damn it.

As soon as we went below deck, I started

making plans on how I could remodel the main cabin. Nice, fairly open space with easy access to the small galley and the small navigation station.

Great layout for having guests aboard. Two staterooms, one fore and one aft...each with its own head and shower and hanging closets, nice size main salon for get-togethers if the weather doesn't permit a cockpit party, nice access from the galley to pass food and drinks up to the cockpit, ya gotta think about these things.

I can already imagine my lovely crew-members naked body lying on the master stateroom berth.

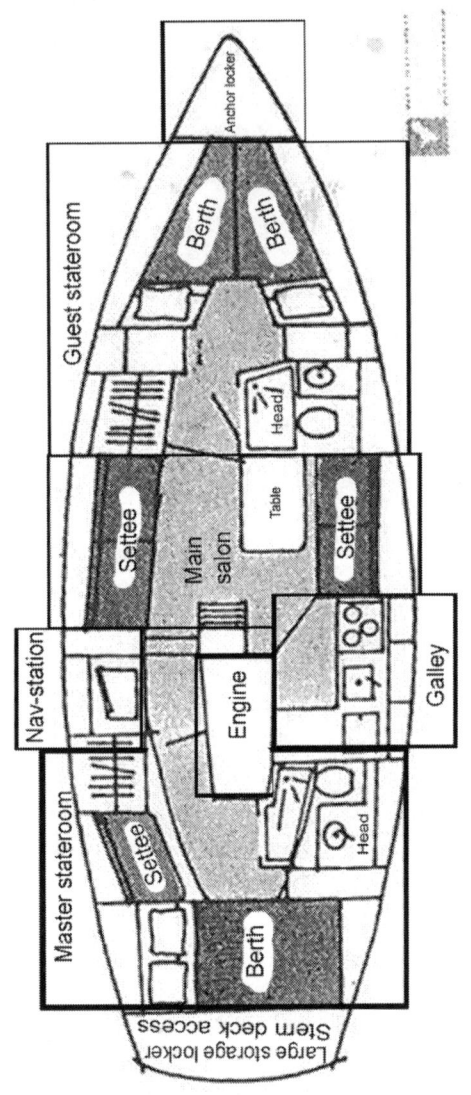

Below deck layout

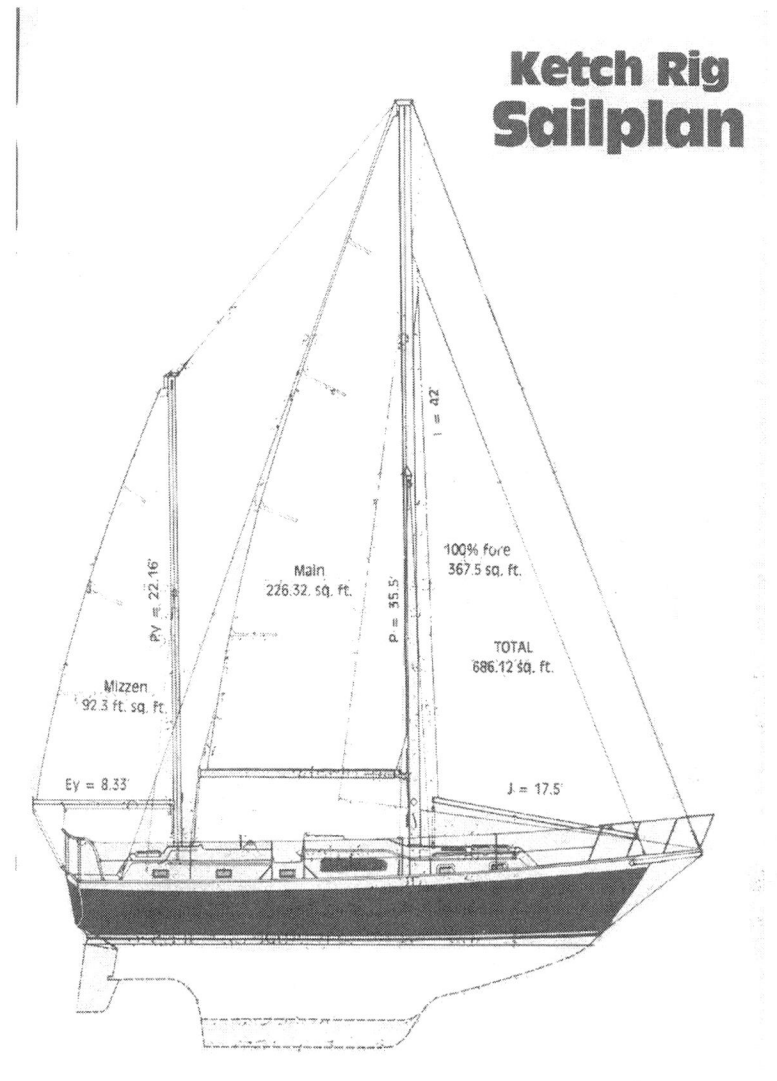

Eric and Dotty related more of their exciting sailing adventures on the Inter-coastal waterway and in the Bahamas and expanded about the merits of *Marigold* with the shoal draft swing keel. She would go where some smaller boats couldn't...safely, and with the swing keel lowered was stable enough for the open ocean.

Both sales reps showed up at the same time to discover that we had already done a bunch of their work for them. After spending hours with the Ericsons and chatting, I was ready to take the next step and get a hold of my surveyor and schedule a time to do an inspection ASAP. Lowe's boatyard has cranes large enough to bring *Marigold* into dry-dock for the inspection and Eric said they could be ready almost on a moments notice...great!

I liked *Marigold,* and I liked the owners. Eric told some pretty corny jokes, however. After some haggling over some of the equipment involving some give and take, on both sides, we came to an agreement with some contingencies depending on the outcome of the inspections and trials...Eric will throw in the tender after making a big deal about getting robbed.

The required contracts were signed and deposits made—I think I need a drink.

I really needed to know if there was going to be any way possible for this boat to fit in my price range without a good deal more expense.

I couldn't wait to call Kathy, "I think this is going to be our boat" I tried to withhold my excitement. "I made an offer to Eric, and we came to a fair agreement with contingencies depending on and based on the results of the inspection. At least they didn't say no."

"You really think this is the one? Does she have most all of the equipment we will need to sail safely?" Kathy inquired cautiously, "Will you have to spend a lot more money to get whatever she's lacking?"

Huh, oh...all of a sudden it is "will you have to" in this conversation. A clue as to commitment maybe?

"I will know a lot more after the sea trials and get her under sail. Need to check out the instruments, loran navigation, radar unit, and running rigging, etc. One thing for sure will be a dinghy and engine unless I can get them thrown in as part of a deal"

"You better call me tomorrow night and plan on spending a lot of time answering some questions there skipper," Kathy said as we hung up.

I went to sleep with the thought of sailboats running through my mind jumping over channel buoys.

I had made arrangements with Henry Pickersgill, as the yacht surveyor and consultant, to do the survey. In order for everything to come together, it was set for the next day at 10:00 a.m. So far, everyone I have met on this trip has been great to work with.

INSPECTION
15

Everyone showed up on time for my big day. Henry Pickersgill, the yacht surveyor and consultant, was very professional and looked like a yachtsman should look, tan and fit, about my size, a little older than me and quick to smile. Of course, Robert was there to keep things legal, and I must say he has been a big help. Looking out for us.

The skies were overcast, as I'm told is the case a lot this time of year, with brief showers on and off. I am struggling with the words to describe my feelings about the entire event coming together over the next several hours.

This boat, these people, this marina in this coastal town, the overcast and slight breeze with an off and on drizzle, the various birds expressing their opinion adding to the background of watery sounds, the sights, and aroma are almost overwhelming. My mind envisioned and wondered what it would really be like. I am not disappointed.

Even back in my horsey cowboy days, I would go out to the barn, chew on a straw of alfalfa, and just breath. Strange huh?

Everyone is in a good mood and enjoying the entire experience...more corny jokes told by Eric...they really are nice people.

If everything checks out, we will do the sea trials in the afternoon after the haul-out. This is the part I'm looking forward to the most.

Henry, the surveyor, did what I felt was a very comprehensive inspection and took the time to point out important aspects of the survey and what I should expect. He respected and accepted the fact that I was new at this and gave me the benefit of his knowledge. Whatever he's charging is well worth the money.

After the haul-out inspection and during everyone's lunch, I called Kathy to bring her up to date on the progress. "I wish I could be there," I wish she were here too.

"How soon could we make a trip to Florida to sail her if all goes well? Where will we keep her until then? If she needs some work, who would do it? Did we really decide on a name?"

"Shotgun questions going on here," I said, "slow down there mate. I've been thinking about a plan for all of that."

A SAIL ABOARD WALKABOUT

SEA TRIALS
16

The sea trials couldn't start soon enough. This is what it's all about...getting under-sail on what is possibly to become my new yacht. The jellyfish and seagulls in my stomach are raging at this point.

The haul-out went smooth thanks to the skill of one of Lowe's expert crane operators. *Marigold* looks so much bigger out of the water. Eric and Henry gave me several pointers about the swing keel. Interesting to see it in operation up close. Henry keeps hitting the hull with a mallet in several locations and inspected the rudder and thru-hull fittings.

Henry felt the haul-out inspection went well and couldn't detect any significant problems that would have a negative effect on *Marigold* being a sound boat and recommended we proceed with the sea trial and continue the inspection. That was good enough for me! Let's go...cast off the lines.

Eric skillfully maneuvered *Marigold* out of the marina and into the channel to take us out of Manatee Pocket toward the St. Lucie River. The St. Lucie inlet/ outlet to the Atlantic is very shallow and can be difficult to maneuver so everyone thought it best to do the trials on the river. OK by me.

We tested my new best friend...the autopilot, gotta love the autopilot. Henry started the Perkins 4-108 diesel up to full RPM and the top speed of *Marigold*. No sign of overheating or rough running. Speed was underwhelming but seemed to be plenty of power if needed to get out of tight situations (put to good use later in the adventure).

I named the Perkins diesel Carl...Carl Perkins...get it? For the under-educated, Carl was a country western singer.

I named the autopilot Matt because it took over the helm when needed. OK, did you get this one...Matt Helm. Jeeez! Really?

Time to hoist some sail. I can't get over my new found love for the autopilot.

The boys had me doing most of the work to get the sails ready to hoist and actually sail this boat. I wouldn't have wanted it any other way. I wanted to experience the proper steps that needed to be taken and in what order...basically it's like Destiny only way bigger.

I was glad to have such a competent crew, and we even got to run up the mizzen sail for a short while. Three sheets to the wind as it were. Destiny didn't have the benefit of roller furling for the genoa like *Marigold* does...wow! *Marigold* is also equipped with a genoa, which is a much larger type of jib. Nice upgrade.

The entire time surveyor Henry was inspecting everything and asking lots of questions of Eric while taking pages of notes. I started to get worried, but he was just doing an outstanding job as it turned out.

I couldn't wait to tell Kathy about my two new best friends...Matt and Carl.

Finally my turn at the helm

Sea trial time is drawing to a close. I am having so much fun I didn't want to head back to the dock, but at the same time, I wanted to get things going to proceed to the purchase portion of this fine mini-yacht. I'm sold! Since this is going to be a cash purchase, and all the involved parties were already here, it should be simple.

APRIL 15, 1991
17

"Let's do this!"

The closing went very smooth since everything had already been agreed upon. Eric did give up the tender along with several other items that weren't deal breakers one way or another. Damn, you'd thought I was pulling all his teeth.

Eric and Dot said early on that it would be hard for them to turn their beloved *Marigold* over to a stranger. "We've owned this boat since she was new and have had many years of pleasure on her." Today they said…"We really like you and are so glad you and Kathy will be her new masters and hope you get the same enjoyment of sailing as we have." I'm getting kinda teary-eyed at this point. "We hope to run into you and Kathy in the islands next winter. We're really excited for you."

I told them, "You guys are my heroes and are living the life I hope to experience, and you are still doing it, and now I'm gonna do it!" Lot's of hugs going on here. I love it. We had actually become friends during this short time. Just gotta love sail-boaters.

Henry advised me on a few minor things that the Ericsons had agreed to take care of utilizing Lowe's boatyard for the repairs and replacement of some older seals that Henry noticed during the trials.

Eric and Dotty had already removed all of the

personal items and just waiting for their rep to hand me the keys, and I am the new owner. Whew!! What a ride to this point and now the fun work begins.

There was talk about having a group dinner to celebrate, but I needed to have some alone time with my new purchase so I could sit aboard, wonder, and think about what I had just done. I keep imagining Kathy lying naked on the berth in the master stateroom while at anchor at some remote island. My mind slips into the gutter sometimes...a lot.

I called Kathy since she was still at work "Hey sweetheart it's a done deal," I briefly told her, "and I will call you this evening with all the details. Gotta run now, got some things to do before they run me outta here."

But, but...," she pleaded. "Oh...OK, fantastic. I can't wait!"

TAKING POSSESSION
18

I would have loved to sleep on board what is now *Walkabout,* at least in my mind, but she is docked in an area of the marina that didn't allow overnight stays, and they were getting ready to close the gates soon. I stayed on the docks as long as they would let me, thinking back to all of the challenges we had to overcome to get to this point...quite a trip to even get this far. My entire being is smiling with pride. At the same time thinking, "what the hell have I done!?"

Across Hobie Sound from Lowe's was a waterfront bar and restaurant called Pirates Cove. It has an unobstructed view of Lowe's marina and *Walkabout* at rest in her slip. I'm thinking, "what a perfect place to have a celebration dinner for myself."

I decided to go all out and get the steak and lobster sit by a window and continue living in my fantasy world while looking across the water at what has become our *Walkabout* of the future.

The sun was well on its way to setting, and the lights of the harbor were starting to come on that gives the harbor a glow that kind of reminded me of a Christmas tree and lights.

This magic scene took me back to childhood and getting up before anyone one else on Christmas morning and sneaking out to the living room and gaze at the presents under and around the tree. They would always leave the tree lights on for Santa. Mom and Dad, truly great parents, had spent most of the night setting up toys and stuff for my brothers and me. I could see the toys but couldn't go out and play with them--yet. Jeeez!

I wish I didn't have to head home tomorrow, but at the same time, I knew the quicker I got things accomplished there, the sooner I could be back in Florida. I started making a list of the things I need Lowe's to do that weren't part of the sales contract.

For sure I need the name of a good painter to take care of the name change once I got the coastguard registration filed and cleared. Superstitious about changing the name of a boat? A big part of this goal is to go on Walkabout, so that meant its name had to be changed. *(I should have investigated this a little more.)* It's got to be a western style of lettering across the stern of course.

"Hey sweetheart, what an exciting day I had! I took lots of pictures and an hour of video. I can't wait to show you. Eric and Dot gave us a video tour. Nice couple."

"And I can't wait to see them! Please tease me! I want to know everything you got to do. Did you get a chance to sail her? Are you going to come back to Colorado or hop on your little boat and sail away?" she said with a joking excitement in her voice.

"It has crossed my mind," I retorted, "but I need a crew to follow my every command, and you're it, my dear."

"Remember, just don't fall overboard, sweetheart," she said. She only lets me live my fantasy so far before slapping me back to reality. "Have you ever read Mutiny On The Bounty or The Cane mutiny? If not, I suggest you read them before our first trip."

"Marigold really is the one I've been looking for, and I have some wonderful ideas to improve her to suit our needs and comfort. I need you here to offer suggestions, but that will have to wait. I'm thinking we can plan a trip for this May for a few weeks to check things out and sail a bit. What do ya think? I've already envisioned you naked in the 'master' stateroom berth, and you looked yummy."

"Yummy? Sounds wonderful to me," she purred.

"I'll see you tomorrow night," I said.

I met with Mr. Lowe the next morning and went over my list of items that my surveyor had suggested needed to be repaired and to combine it with the list that was part of the sales contract. Eric Ericson had already talked to Mr. Lowe about what he was paying for so it would be nice to do everything at the same time. By this time Mr. Lowe said I could call him David...nice.

David will work up prices and time frames and give me a call to get my permission to start the work.

On the return trip home, I just couldn't resist telling everyone on the plane about my recent purchase and ambitions of sailing the high seas and exotic islands. Bragging??...you better believe it!

MOVING ABOARD
19

Taking the steps to fulfill a major dream is a life aphrodisiac. Every day is a "rush" of adrenaline. It is a warming thrill to reach this point, closer to realizing this sailing fantasy, and at the same time taking time to enjoy the other important people and things that I couldn't enjoy while operating the business. My business was also a dream come true, and now it has given me the opportunity to proceed to the next one. The business was a fantastic ride with many lessons, getting thrown off and then gettin' back on again.

More time with my wonderful daughter! I can spend more time with all of my various animal friends, and equally important, continue to develop a hopefully lasting relationship with Kathy. We have so much fun doing things together, and the sex is great!

The month was spent planning a trip to Florida and move aboard *Walkabout* for a few weeks. Now we're almost ready to go. May seemed like the best time to do it, not too hot in Florida yet, and mostly clear weather is forecast. Perfect!

Kathy and I spent many hours, almost every evening, developing our plan of attack. Our lists included everything to take that would stay on the boat plus what we needed for the several weeks we planned to stay aboard...let's see...shorts, more shorts, and a lot of t-shirts, deck shoes, and socks, etc.

I have been spending my time ordering items

and equipment that would be needed to just enjoy some short sailing trips. First on the list was *Walkabouts* very own American flag.

I was absolutely floored as the list of items grew...put an entirely new meaning to the term "batteries not included."

Speaking of batteries, I also requisitioned a 12-volt converter to convert to a 110-volt outlet. I plan on using the 110-volt to recharge the computer and printer in addition to the rechargeable batteries, or any small electrical 110-volt power item, while anchored out. A really great item to have aboard. Lot's of uses.

Navigation equipment was the easiest to order, and I get to play with all the neat stuff in the meantime. I wish I could afford a new GPS, but I'll have to give the loran a chance due to the expense. Chart-books for south Florida and the Bahamas, Weems and Plath Deluxe Navpak includes everything needed to plot, chart, and track a course on charts...oh, the places I am taking us on these maps were a lot more fun than playing the Pirates game on my computer which I also did a lot of.

(I can't say how many hours I've spent sailing that little pirate ship around the Caribbean blowing stuff up.)

The real Florida Keys and then the Bahamas were going to be reached in the near future, but I won't be blowing anything up. *I keep hearing the song Kokomo in my head.*

I have been giving Kathy volumes of material to read about sailing and to prepare her for life onboard a boat. Everything from how to abandon ship to how to avoid getting sunburn on naked body parts. I think I should have included more about sea-sickness--cause and effect kind of stuff, AND, how the close quarters of being on a boat for days on end can affect a relationship.

"Have you been reading all the stuff I've given you sweetheart?

"I sure have skipper, most of it, and there will be time on the boat to read also," came her timid reply. "that way I can look at what I am reading about."

Damn it! I hate it when she's right!

"Uh...OK," damn it! "but it's important stuff ya know!" hoping to drive home a point.

I spend a lot of time transferring more of my music from records and eight-tracks onto cassette tapes...we gotta have our tunes. *(Yes, you read that correctly.)* Recorded lots of movies also. VHS.

We shipped boxes of all the boat gear we accumulated over the past weeks to Florida. Lowe's Boatyard said they would receive and hold the boxes until we arrived.

Arrangements were made to have all of our critters cared for while we were gone complete with house-sitters...no worries.

PORT SALERNO
20

May 21st, we arrived in Port Salerno before noon, like two kids getting out of school for the summer. Kathy was very impressed with Port Salerno and the area in general, and couldn't wait to get to the boatyard and see *Walkabout* first hand. David had put *Walkabout* in a slip that allowed us to stay aboard overnights and work on the boat.

I intentionally led Kathy down the dock that was behind where I saw *Walkabout* docked.

This is the first time Kathy has seen her. It was so thrilling to watch the look on her face when we walked up behind *Walkabout.* The painter I had contracted to change the new name (the curse) did a fantastic job.

WALKABOUT. Golden, co.

She was so excited and exclaimed, "It's even better than I imagined sweetheart. She has our name on it, how great is that!! God, I love it."

"I want you to scream that out a little later tonight too," I said.

I took the honor of being the proud tour guide by taking her around the deck first and then the cockpit to increase her anxiousness to check it out below. She has a way with these sparkling eyes.

"There seems to be more room than I thought. This is so cool!"

Our small shipment of gear and possessions had arrived, and Lowe's kept them safe as promised.

"Where do we start skipper?"

"First things first," pointing to the boxes that were marked bedding and clothes I said to Kathy, "we need to sort the things we need for sleeping aboard tonight first, and then stow all of the other boxes below deck. I plan on taking the crew out for a romantic dinner across the bay at Pirates Cove and then coming back here and have my way with the said crew."

It is exciting to find new places to store all the items we brought and give Kathy a chance to practice her 'nesting skills'. Uh-oh...I had forgotten I wasn't allowed to ever use that term again.

After getting to the point of satisfied with our progress unpacking, we showered and dressed in our best yachty looking outfits consisting of t-shirts with some kind of nautical symbols, our best yachty looking shorts, and cool deck shoes. Kathy held her long blonde hair in a ponytail and was looking great. She wears very little or no makeup at all, I love it!

"We're almost official sailors! We own a boat!"

"We won't be official until after we get out on the water and that will be happening soon."

We managed to get the same table that I enjoyed when I was there before. It has the view of David Lowe's Boatyard and *Walkabout*, across the shimmering water.

Kathy grabbed my hand, and looked at me and said "We're here...we're heading into the next level of this exciting adventure," sporting a warming smile on her face, "I can't believe we are really here! How romantic is this!?!

Of course, I agreed because it was precisely the same way I was feeling. It took a lot of work to get to this point, and WOW...it's just like I had imagined so far.

Arriving back at *Walkabout* we enjoyed a smoke in the cockpit listening to some Jimmy Buffet. *(Skippers note; we never smoked below deck, and do quit before heading to the islands).* I know candles are not a good idea on a boat, but we couldn't resist having one lit on the cockpit table while enjoying a glass or two of red wine, after all--this is a special moment.

There were only a couple of other boats that were occupied, and we appreciated the alone time to actually soak in this entire evening and experience the feeling of what this boating life can be like. We soon started feeding each other's imagination with thoughts of quiet anchorages in the islands, already planning the next steps on this adventure. Right now we are going to enjoy the forbidden fruits of *this* step as long as we can.

The marina provided some nice well kept shower rooms so we shared one to save water, your back can never be too clean.

I led Kathy down the companionway into the main salon and changed the music to our favorite Enya tape. I asked Kathy not to move. I had turned a light on in the forward cabin to provide only enough light to heighten the mood and provide a sexy dark outline of our soon to be naked bodies, counting on the main cabin curtains doing their job.

This is it-this is one of the experiences we have been planning on, counting on, happening. This is going to be the first of what will be many romantic encounters aboard *Walkabout*. With the entire surreal environment going on around us, we let ourselves be consumed in the moment, as it should be.

Our bodies were becoming soaked with sweat

from the Florida humidity and our passion rising with the soothing sounds of Enya playing in the background.

There wasn't much natural water movement of *Walkabout* but just enough to add to the motions and emotions going on in this cabin.

So far I'm liking this "romance of the sea" stuff.

Waking up this morning, I still couldn't believe I was here. I spent several minutes looking around the stateroom to commit this moment to my memory. I looked at Kathy still comfortably asleep in the berth and appeared to have a smile on her face. I always rise early and make coffee and then proceeded to the cockpit to enjoy the first cup and a cigarette as skipper. A glorious day, even with a little overcast! I'm in the zone here--giddy actually!

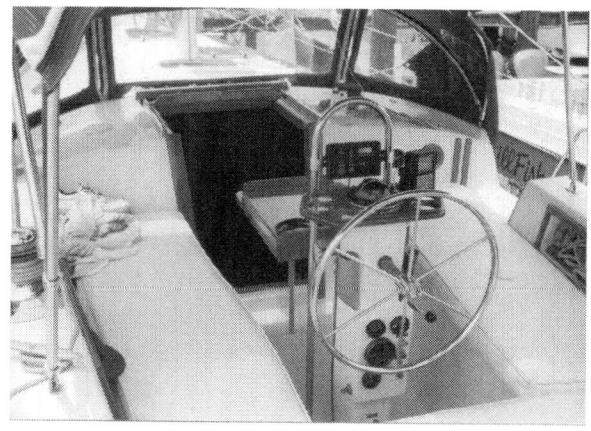

This cockpit is our "living" room.

Kathy finally pulled herself out of bed after a short while and joined me in the cockpit stating, "How cool is this! The gentle rocking of the boat made me want to sleep in, but the smell of fresh coffee made me want to get up, the coffee won."

We thoroughly enjoyed our first morning and looked forward to many, many more. I have trouble putting into words worthy enough to describe how this waterfront and bay looks and sounds. Just like in the movies!

Close your eyes and evoke some thoughts of the gentle sounds water makes. The various sweet songs of the birds excited about their new day, the activities of aquatic life breaching the waters surface, the refreshing feel and smell of a soft breeze, the aroma of fresh coffee, and the exciting sound of the person you love greeting you, "Good morning skipper, are we still afloat?" Corny? Yes! It's my book, and I'll be as corny as I want!

"Big day we have planned. Need to get the boat in proper order and do an inventory of provisions and gear."

We have made plans for a couple of friends to fly down and join us this coming weekend and help us enjoy our first real trip on *Walkabout*. We'll glide down the Inter-coastal Waterway to Palm Beach. We have sailed with Ed and Trixie many times aboard Destiny on Chatfield lake so they would be an ideal first crew, I give orders, and they would ignore me and have another beer, perfect! It's very important to know how your crew will behave in a situation.

Having our lists in hand we headed out to the nearest West Marine store *(I love that place and could spend all day there)* to buy the gear needed to get our yacht ready to receive guest and, at some point, get underway. New life jackets, new lines of various sizes, bumpers, fiberglass wax and cleaners--just a lot of stuff. If you've ever owned a boat or an RV, you know what I mean. So far I'm still within budget, and the car is loaded.

Back to Lowe's to unload so I can get started stowing the gear and Kathy can go to the local Win Dixie grocery store for food provisions and cleaning supplies. Kathy is going to clean and disinfect the entire interior of *Walkabout* so everything starts fresh.

One of the most frustrating things about boats and RV's is trying to find items you've stored. I spent a good part of the cockpit time this morning drawing a layout of the entire boat to show all of the possible storage spaces and lettered them. I went through the entire alphabet and then started double letters, AA, etc.

I brought along my little portable IBM laptop computer equipped with up-to-date DOS operating system with the Lotus spreadsheet program and a portable printer. Both laptop and printer were battery operated. Every item and it's quantity, no matter how small, was entered into the computer along with it's assigned storage space number or letter.

The information can then be sorted by compartment, item name and quantity, and item category, for example; Food, green beans, located in "A," "0" quantity. Time to restock. This inventory is done right down to all the nuts and bolts. Just do a printout of items needed to buy on the next shopping trip.

(This system alone saved me/us a great deal of time and frustration over the years, and it was easy to maintain.)

At sea, we learned how little a person really needs.
(Make that get by on).

I try to be prepared, just like being on a road trip, you better have the stuff needed to jury rig almost anything that breaks--enough to get you thru an emergency anyway. That's gotta cover a lot of stuff on a boat that may be miles from land or help.

Kathy arrived, and we unloaded a car full of provisions that would get us thru the next several days hopefully.

The provisioning process went better than expected with the storage system I designed. Everything had a place, *AND WE BOTH KNOW* where these things are located. None of this "Honey, do you know where the other bottle of margarita mix is?"

She voiced her approval, "This computer idea is really nice, skipper. We need something like this at home, I can't find anything in my own kitchen. How about a sandwich for lunch to get us through to dinner? I have all your favorite fixings, it would be perfect to eat our first meal in the cockpit, and I got your milk. Put on a Buffett tape for some tunes." She has this smile on her face as she speaks. I like it.

"Yes please, that sounds really nice."

There are just so many firsts on this trip it's hard to actually paint a picture or choose the best.

We are having our first meal aboard and having it in the cockpit. This is our living room with walls that display an ever-changing view, a dining room, a patio, and a place of solace.

I asked Kathy, "Tell me about your shopping experience at a new store in a new town. I know they have some things here that we don't have at home. Did you find any treasures?"

"God yes, it was interesting, and I love the fruit and vegetable department. I know you're not into the healthy stuff, so I just got myself a small supply. Even at that, I barely had enough room in the fridge. I hope that built-in freezer under the nav station works. Can we check it out on this trip?"

"Yes! Good idea! If we're going to be taking steaks and other meats for four people it better work. Looking at the condition of the fridge, I'm not sure where to put the beer."

"Well, you better get on it cowboy, uh, I mean skipper."

CAST OFF THE BOWLINES
21

The next several days were spent perfecting our storage system and making unending lists. That lead to more shopping trips for gear we need to get our yacht ready for guests to come aboard...at the very least make her sea-worthy. This is the first test of all the reasons I have given myself, and my friends, to justify me going "all-in" for this venture.

We have had the urge, but not yet the nerve, to attempt a trip up the river to anchor out for an evening.

I said to Kathy, "I have to know that we can handle the basic functions of this ship before subjecting our friends to the chaos of a first trip and looking incompetent to boot. You know how Ed is."

She got that mischievous look on her face and nodded approval, "Let's do it, I can't think of a better time, and I'm anxious to know how she feels out in the water!"

May 22nd '91 and we are as ready as we'll ever be considering our schedule. Keeping in mind we wanted this to be like being real sailors, so we planned our attack as though we were really heading offshore. Remembering our earlier lessons on the effects of tides, we even checked the tide schedule to time our departure. Around 10:00am the tide would be about mid-way rising, and that would give us plenty of prep time to cast off and put us out in some shallow areas on a rising tide, even though our shoal draft keel would still have had plenty of depth. I am practicing to be a real sailor. Never set a schedule that can't be changed.

9:50 we are ready to go. I start the 'ol Perkins auxiliary and let her warm up and check the gauges for normal operation. Satisfied that everything was working I take a look around deck to make sure everything was stowed and properly lashed down.

"**Cast off the bowlines** there matey." I boldly commanded beginning our maiden voyage.

"Aye-aye skipper," came the reply.

Kathy stood ready with the boat hook to keep us away from the dock and ready to push us back, I cast off the stern lines and slipped *Walkabout* into reverse..."We're free of land sweetheart," as we gently backed out of the slip with Kathy ready at the bow.

Once clear of the dock Kathy pulled up the dock bumpers and stored them as I nudged *Walkabout* into forward and we slowly motored out of the marina. I know the look on our faces had to be that of excited fear.

The staff at Lowe's were manning the radio so that if we got into trouble, they could advise...bless them for that bit of security.

We were really feeling the excitement of the moment.

"Remember how you felt when you would see a sailboat heading out on the water and wondered, "where are they going? How great would that be?" I wonder if anyone is watching us and thinking the same thing about us," Kathy said in a very surprisingly relaxed tone.

"I was just thinking the same thing and starting to feel so proud and at ease that we can do this. You're doing great by the way...thanks," I replied.

Leaving Manatee Pocket would be considered going downstream and then entering the St Lucie

River would be considered going upstream so leaving the pocket means the red channel buoys should be kept on the left, or port side of the boat, and entering the river would be considered going upstream, therefore the red buoys should be on the right. "Red right return" always rule '#1' when in marked channels.

We made sure we followed the proper buoys out of the pocket and into the St Lucie River. Entering into the main channel, we decide to put our "hoist the mainsail" practice into action. Hereafter called just "hoist the main."

Beautiful clear day with a light off-shore breeze and no other boat traffic, so it's time to put our skills to work. I performed a quick check of the deck gear and lines as Kathy was readying the main for her first breath of air with her new crew aboard.

Perfect! With the main holding the light air in her graceful shape after some adjustment of the main sheet. I shut down Carl Perkins, and we were instantly mesmerized by the peaceful silence of *Walkabout* gliding thru the water under sail power alone. This is it! This is one of those moments we have been working toward...wonderful! "Let's run out the genoa and see what that's like," I said. We were only going a short distance, but I craved the thrill running under sail.

I couldn't wait to approach the draw bridge where A1A crosses the river and request an opening after setting the radio on channel 9. Kathy wasn't aware that we would be doing this maneuver, so the look on her face was priceless. Alerting Kathy to what needed to be done I cranked up the Perkins and then came about into the wind so we could roll in the genoa and drop and secure the main. After hailing the bridge the proper three times, including, "this is the northbound sailing vessel *Walkabout* requesting an opening."

He responded, *"Walkabout,* we have you in sight skipper, and as soon as your closer, we will raise the bridge."

"This is sailing vessel *Walkabout* standing by thank you."

The bridge keeper blew the horn to signal bridge traffic and started lowering the gates. After traffic has stopped, the bascule bridge started making it's way open for us.

*"**That** is so amazing...thrilling actually,"* Kathy said. "Feels like a 'show of respect' in a way, for what we are doing...maybe wishing they could be doing it themselves someday...that was very cool!"

"I hope they do get their chance," I said, thinking about how wonderful I am feeling right now just doing this much. "Nice job with the sails by the way. What a crew!"

"This is *Walkabout* and we are clear...thank you very much...this is our first time so thanks for making it so easy, have a nice day."

"Have a nice sail skipper," came the reply.

I noticed a red bilge pump light come on just before we dropped sail as we approached the bridge. It didn't stay on very long it seems so I figured it was just some water that was already in the bilge and just made its way to the pump. I was somewhat correct.

Not long after we raised the main and ran out the genoa after passing the bridge, the bilge light came on again. OK, I'm thinking the same thoughts as before only this time I felt I should think more about where the water was coming from. *WOW, we get to practice our disaster-at-sea drill...this is an unfortunate opportunity to learn...damn it!*

I had Kathy man the helm and pointed her in the direction I needed her to head. I quickly went below to take a look in the bilge and observed water being sucked up by the pump. The pump was keeping up with it fine, but the water still came back...seemed to be coming from forward, another 'damn it' with an added 'W T F?' *(abbreviated sailor talk here)* I went above to check on our progress and position. Kathy was doing just great.

We were still a few miles from the anchorage that I had planned on staying tonight.

Heading into the forward cabin, I lifted the hatch to the bilge and to my shock, I could see water running down the V of the bow, not a gushing amount but still a steady flow. Now I'm getting worried and need to investigate this more and come up with a plan or abandon ship.

I explained the situation to the crew as calmly as I could, "We need to drop sails, stop the boat and heave to so I can get a better look for the source of the water."

We had the Perkins running and in neutral while I went forward to check bilge. Strange...no running water and now the pump had turned off. We bobbed around for some time, and there was no change.

"Bilge still dry," I announced from below. Seems to me like the V in the bow stayed moist, however. "Maybe it was coming from our fresh water tank," I added.

As we got underway again, I ran out the genoa and

then checked the bilge for the leak, and sure enough, we were taking on water...again! A slow leak, but a water intrusion just the same.

As we approached the authorized anchorage area, we picked our spot and motored into position and dropped anchor, 'dropping the hook' as it's called, going through our practice procedure of setting the anchor. With around 10 feet of water below our bottom meant I should have about 120 feet of scope, also known as rode. The scope should be 7-10 feet of scope to 1 foot of depth plus the distance from the bow to water. The more chain you have, the less anchor line you need to let out. Another essential factor to consider when setting the hook is the tide. The incoming/outgoing tide will change your depth, so you should allow for these changes.

I busied myself securing all sheets and lines and making sure *Walkabout* was comfortable in her new location. Nice to actually see all that practice pay off on our effort to become sailors. I had identified two landmarks to confirm we weren't drifting.

When everything settled down we had a chance to stop...take a look around...see how far we have come...and then broke into a couple of the biggest smiles you've ever seen. Here we are...anchored out on our very own pristine looking sailboat, on a beautiful sunny Florida afternoon at a heightened level of enjoyment and excitement, and then we experienced the calm...the calm of what this boating lifestyle is supposed to be all about. We were challenged, and we met that challenge, and in doing so, it took away a good deal of our initial fears and gave us a little more confidence in our abilities.

Recap of our first day away from the safety of the dock;

- ✓ Enjoyed morning coffee and cigarette in the cockpit and planned the final steps to casting off the bowlines and heading out.
- ✓ Proper castoff and motoring out of the marina and into the St. Lucie river without looking incompetent along the way.
- ✓ Experienced a water leak somewhere in the hull and decided to continue the trip. Maybe not the smartest thing to do but it worked.
- ✓ Sailing upriver with the genoa and mainsail.
- ✓ Passing thru a drawbridge without being de-masted in the process.
- ✓ Setting anchor and settling into the late afternoon quiet of our anchorage, and feeling proud of our accomplishments.

With the peacefulness of the moment, I wanted to enter the day's events into the ship's log. A quiet time at the nav station to relive the sights and sounds and put everything on record. "Maybe someday I'll write a book," I whispered to myself while flashing a grin.

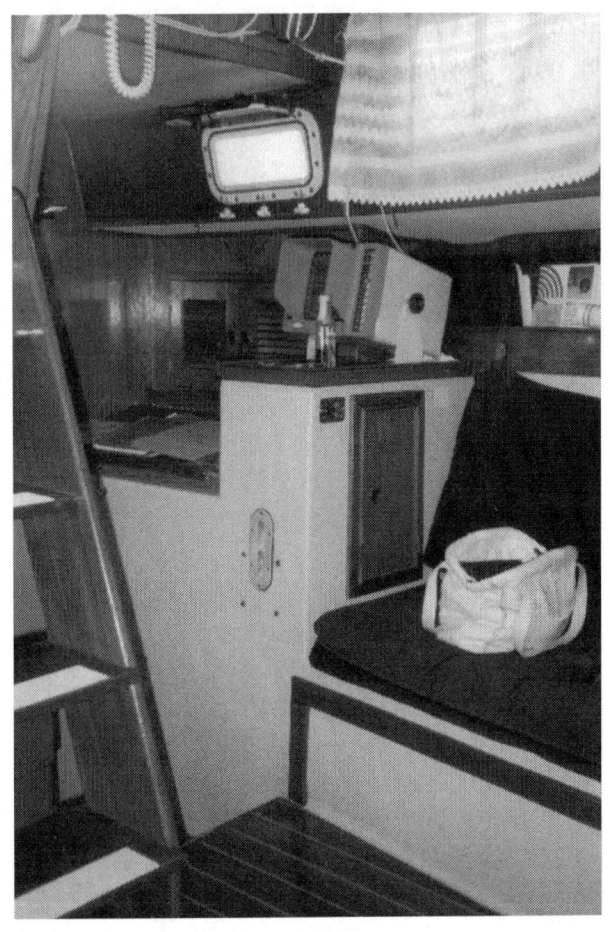

Walkabout navigation station...my office...I love it! Note my best friend...the 12-mile radar. The ladder leads into the cockpit.

FIRST ANCHOR OUT
22

Time to open that special bottle of wine that was planned just for this occasion. The wine was cheap, but the experience was priceless!

"A toast to the crew of *Walkabout* and all of our accomplishments today," I proposed. We clinked our plastic glasses as music by Jimmy Buffett's *'Why Don't We Get Drunk And Screw'* played in the background. Sounded tempting to me as you might have guessed! However, it's time to debrief about the day's events.

"I know you might think it strange but I'm glad we encountered the leak problem today," I said. "This could have happened anywhere or anytime we were offshore and not have the comfort of knowing that help was nearby. We worked as a team to get things under control, a good test for us. How about you...how do you feel?"

After taking a few moments to organize her thoughts, "The entire trip was very exhilarating, and I was surprised at how comfortable *Walkabout* is under sail...loved it," she said with all the excitement of the bright eyed-little girl she was at that moment. "But, I must add that when you said we were taking on water, I started to get a little scared." Both of us laughing so much our sides hurt.

We poured another glass of wine, and Kathy was anxious to give the galley a test under 'out of marina conditions.' Like most sailboats, the galley was one step down from the main salon and a very small, one person kind of space with its own porthole. *Yeah!* All the cook needed to do was turn 45 degrees one way or the other to access everything in the galley. You were actually trapped on three and a half sides, and that keeps you from falling when in unstable seas or offshore or in a drunken state due to too much grog or having found that extra bottle of margarita mix.

Cozy galley. Note the Ruffles.

"Our evening meal is going to be that of the extremely rare exotic seafood called Sloppy Joe, served open face or with a topper bun along with your favorite Ruffles chips and a stein of milk. This little galley is so cool to work in, at least for these simple meals," she seemed to be ecstatic about the experience.

I could smell the alluring aroma of Sloppy Joe cooking as I decided to do some minor deck chores, including checking the anchor. The main anchor was a plow type, also known as CQR, and Eric had told me it sets very well on most types of bottoms. *Walkabout* has a second Danforth type of anchor mounted on the stern in case it was needed depending on the kind of bottom you are anchoring in. Just for peace of mind, I decided we will deploy it off the bow after dinner so we could sleep better tonight. Laying out two anchors was very good practice for us as a crew. This allowed for good swing room and twice the holding. Make sure the "bitter end" of your anchor lines are tied off and secure. Note to self; buy another Danforth backup anchor for the bow.

> *"Anchor as though you plan to stay for weeks,*
> *even   if you intend to leave in an hour."- Tommy*
> *Moran*

While standing out on the bow pulpit after checking the anchor, I had a chance to take the time to look around, I want to take in all the sights and sounds and smells of my surroundings as much as I could. So far, this is all that I had imagined it would be. The shore lights were starting to come on and added a romantic effect to it all as well as the comfort of knowing civilization was close by.

Looking toward the stern from the bow makes me realize how much boat there really is. Man, I sure like this deck layout.

The gourmet dinner, complete with our usual candle and wine, was served in the cockpit in grand style as the sun set on this glorious day. We were starting to get comfortable with our surroundings.

I asked Kathy to take a stroll with me around the deck after dinner, "Can you believe that it was only six months ago we were dreaming about doing this very thing?" she smiled and grabbed my arm as we took it all in glowing in our success.

"Time for another practice lesson," I announced. "We are going to set the Danforth anchor at about 20 to 40 degrees off the starboard bow from our first anchor. First, we will slowly motor up and to the right of the first anchor, lower the Danforth, and let *Walkabout* drift back with the proper amount of scope and set the anchor, thus giving us a "V" shape in relation to our anchors. I want a comfortable nights sleep, and this should give us that luxury."

Kathy understood the concept right away since we had used it on Destiny several times, so the "crew" was put into action to make it happen.

A little more wine and another relaxing stroll around the deck and we were ready to settle in for a night of romance on the high seas knowing our small yacht was safe and secure, gently rocking with our twin hooks and the anchor light glowing. A wonderfully sensuous evening unfolded as we totally enjoyed the benefits of all our hard work.

There weren't any hot air balloons lifting off from the shore, but it was still a beautiful morning. Very much to my pleasure we were still in the same relative position as we were last night..."The anchors held firm," I proudly announced.

We had planned to sail a little further up the river and spend another night at anchor, but since we are leaking water at times, and expecting guests in a few days, I decided to head back to Lowe's to see if they could repair whatever is leaking. And, do a little more work on some of the things we wanted to change.

I had Kathy motor *Walkabout* up toward the second anchor we deployed as I hauled in the line and had to use the bow roller to break it free of the bottom...it was well set. After Walkabout settled back onto the plow anchor, Kathy slowly motored up to its position as I hauled in the line with its eight feet of chain and tried to break it free from the bottom. I immediately realized the value of the electric windlass *Walkabout* had on her bow. The anchors had set in some pretty sticky mud.

After getting us moving toward the anchor, I had Kathy leave the Perkins running and put the transmission in neutral as I hauled us the rest of the way using the windlass with just enough speed to get us over the anchor as I tied the line off and let the momentum of 28,000 lbs break it free from the bottom. Easy!

The bow pulpit windlass, and Kathy's stern.

The trip back to the dock went so smooth it made us feel like seasoned sailors...a really good feeling I must add. And, the freezer under the nav station seemed to work reasonably well by the way, but seems like it mostly just kept frozen things from thawing too fast.

We arrived back at Lowe's early afternoon after totally enjoying the last few days.

I tracked down David Lowe and explained the bilge problem as best I could. He was pretty perplexed with everything I told him about our test of only taking on water while under sail with the genoa only. He said he will send one of his best techs' down in the morning since we were not taking on water at this time. I don't think he would want us sinking at his dock, so I was OK with that.

A tech named Rick showed up first thing this morning. Rick was about 5'10" and very slender and around 30, just right for working in the tight spaces of boats. Rick, not a boater himself, loves boats and has been doing this for several years. He had a hard time believing my story but said he had an idea that he would like to check out.

I told him we were going to run some errands and go shopping, which is endless, so he would have *Walkabout* to himself for most of the day. "Great!"

When we returned from our shopping trip, Rick was still working on *Walkabout* and had some good news and of course some bad news.

As I'm sure you guessed, the good news is he found the leak, and it didn't appear to be too bad. The bad news is that it will take several days for the repair, once they schedule it, and that wouldn't be for several weeks.

Rick took me to the bow and explained that the rod running from the bow pulpit to the hull at the water line was bent like it had been hit coming into the dock. This has created a crack almost at the waterline. The crack is not big enough to leak water until it's put under pressure and that happens whenever we ran out the genoa.

Damn...that makes sense and explains why it was leaking just at certain times.

"We didn't hit anything when we were out, and the leak started, or showed up anyway, as soon as we left here," I explained. "How could this happen?"

Wisely Rick didn't try to pin blame anywhere and wanted to turn the matter over to David as soon as he could. I understand that. I could see the $$$$ signs adding up here beside my disappointment of possibly having to cancel our plans with our guests.

David came to discuss the matter shortly after Rick left and he pretty much said the same thing. When I told him we didn't hit anything so it must have been done when they moved the boat after the sale, or when they put it in a slip a day before we arrived. "You folks had the boat out last," was all he would say.

The best he could do would be to give me a break on the repair bill since there was no way to prove how it happened. One of my businesses was an auto repair shop..." that scratch wasn't there when we brought the car in!" so I did know where he was coming from. It's fair.

The good news here was he felt it would be OK to take my friends out for a few days as long as we didn't use the genoa.

I briefed Kathy on the meeting with David, so we decided to go ahead with our plans.

There were so many benefits as a result of this trip. Besides getting some real-time sailing experience, we realized how many more things we needed to buy, not only for necessity but for comfort also. Never enough storage I see. No matter what...this is going to be fun, and, I really want to impress Ed and Trixie.

They are assigned the forward cabin suite...did I mention that the forward head has an electric flush? Is that a cool luxury or what?!!

Ed's idea of roughing it is a "Holiday Inn without a pool" so it will be interesting to see how he handles this 'camper like' boat. *Walkabout* does not have AC, only 12-volt power while away for the dock, and no standing in the shower for extended periods using all the hot water.

FIRST GUESTS
23

May 26, 1991;

The day Ed and Trixie arrived, we had *Walkabout* fully provisioned and in pristine condition. There are some high clouds today and no rain in the forecast. It will be a fine day to welcome our guests aboard and get them settled in. We are so proud.

Ed is 5' 6" and was a motorcycle cop for many years, as fearless as they come! We were old drag racing, beer drinking, women chasing high school buddies. These days he is a lieutenant of some kind for the Denver police department. Trixie is as pretty as they come. They have been married for only a couple of years. Trixie is very typical of Ed's taste in women. I think she might have been a stripper at one time.

They are a fun couple to be around, and Trixie and Kathy get along great! Ed and I have put up with each other for almost 30 years so I hope we can get along another couple of days in close quarters. If not I'll throw his ass overboard!!

For starters, I know he will not take to calling me Captain or Skipper. Since Captain is a higher rank than the lowly lieutenant, he will resent my authority, guaranteed!

A sailboat on an ocean needs to be a gentle dictatorship. - A. Long

This is so true, bad things can happen on a boat if instructions (orders) aren't followed! Not always time to say please...see the problem? When we start our trip down the inter-coastal tomorrow, I will just assign Ed to a cockpit seat to hold down the cushion. I've got to milk this 'one-up-man-ship' as long as I can.

I notified the office we were expecting company and asked to send them to our slip when they arrive.

The landlubbers showed up just before noon, and it was so wonderful to welcome them as our first guests. I saw right away that a more detailed instruction will be in order about what not to bring for our future guests. Large suitcases are not welcome!

"I thought we were going to be on a *real yacht*," Ed said as I showed him around.

"This is as close as you'll ever get to one," I replied. "By the way, Ed, I forgot to ask before, you do know how to swim, right?
"What with all the weight you're putting on I'm not sure I have a large enough life jacket to fit you. Is that Rolex waterproof?" The look he gave me is going to be my only answer.

Kathy and I gave our guests a tour of *Walkabout* along with detailed instructions on the proper use of the head (toilet) and how to use the water system. The head in the guest stateroom is electric and really a joy to use. Most heads need to be hand pumped and seems like they need to be repaired often. (*We have lots of rebuild kits onboard.*)

Ed and Trixie were getting settled into the forward stateroom, and their almost empty suitcases were put in the trunk of their rental car. I called a crew meeting in the cockpit to point out our safety equipment, such as the location of our life-jackets, etc., and go over our plans for the next few days.

Ed was ready for a drink, so I had to stall him off. "We are going to move out into the bay and anchor for the evening so you will get an idea of what the boat movement is going to be like. If we can get that part accomplished, without someone falling overboard, we have cocktail plans at this great little restaurant across the bay called Pirate's Cove," I said. That got Ed's attention.

"How are we going to get to the bar if we are sitting out in the water?" Ed asked with a skeptical look on his face.

"See that red thing floating in the water, It's called a dinghy, or tender, or just the inflatable," I said. "We'll row it over to the bar."

"Row?" Ed said. "Who's going to row? Doesn't it have a motor?"

"Not yet! Rowing is what the 'crew' is for," I replied. "I'll handle the navigation."

"Row my ass," came his reply. "I didn't come here to row a rubber boat!"

"Only the guy who isn't rowing has time to rock the boat."
- Jean-Paul Sartre

Seems we are about to have a mutiny before we even leave the dock!

With the boat name being *Walkabout* Kathy named the tender *Crawlabout*, I thought that was really cute. I had been looking for a used outboard but no luck finding a one before our friends arrived.

"After drinks at Pirate's Cove, we will row back here, grill some steaks, have more cocktails, and then prepare to head off down the inter-coastal waterway to Palm Beach early in the morning."

Ed and Trixie are not their real names but are their actual nicknames. Kathy and I were called Ralph and Alice (after the Honeymooner's characters). We have called each other these names for years. Always fun.

The forward and aft staterooms with heads worked great. Each couple has their own private retreats.

When making plans for our big adventure away from the dock with our guests, I had been advised by Eric, the boatyard, and many locals, that the ST. Lucie inlet could be challenging to navigate for sailboats most of the time. So, it was suggested to head south on the inter-coastal waterway to Palm Beach before attempting to get to the open ocean. With our very minimal experience on the water and the untrained crew, that doesn't follow orders very well, the waterway was our safest bet.

It seems well known that the U.S. Army Corp of Engineers is continuously dredging out the inlet and the waterway due to the constantly shifting sandy bottom. A real problem area is the intersection of the river and the waterway, and that is just the first problem area we will need to navigate.

We planned on taking our time on the trip and have a lot of fun. I am getting excited about the challenge of the whole thing. Of course, the bow leak still gave me cause for concern about heading out to the Atlantic.

Kathy and I opted to keep the bow leak to ourselves before heading out. This way, since Ed's swimming form is a lot like that of an anchor, he won't have a chance to abandon ship before the trip starts.

We had cocktails and lively conversation in the charming Pirates Cove lounge overlooking the bay and *Walkabout* at anchor. We were so proud! So far, everything is fitting into our vision of what this entire adventure should be like.

I'm not sure if there is a law against rowing while intoxicated but if there is...we were guilty. What a blast! Ed just about fell overboard while getting into the dingy. I think his main concern was not getting his Rolex wet.

Back safely aboard *Walkabout,* the female members of the crew started dinner in the galley while Ed took a horizontal position in the cockpit with a fresh cocktail. I fired up the portable gas grill for the steaks that had been marinating all afternoon. I have always been noted for my great steaks, so they seemed fitting for this occasion of "*nautical firsts.*"

After dinner, we enjoyed more cocktails and the company good friends. The quiet peace of the evening setting in has us getting excited about the trip in the morning. We went over some last minute details of what needed to be done before hoisting anchor early in the morning.

DOWN THE INTER-COASTAL
24

May 27, 1991, 9 am;

Under a partly cloudy sky, we weighted anchor to begin our adventure to coincide with the best tide. Its only about 23 miles down the Inter-coastal to Palm Beach and my planned overnight anchorage off Peanut Island. My first planned stop is Peck Lake for a crew and equipment wellness check. Peck is only about six miles down and has a good anchorage and easy access to the Atlantic across the island.

Ed and Trixie were assigned 'watch and learn' duties to see how Kathy and I handled the various boat chores. The trip will take us thru some very narrow and shallow areas and thru one bascule bridge before reaching the lake...only about an hour away. Kathy and I were able to show off our finely honed team-work by getting underway without a problem. It has turned into a beautiful morning. No water leak so far. The first bridge approach and passage went picture perfect. There will be several more along the way.

I chose a beautiful spot in six ft of water and close to the island beach to drop anchor and recheck all deck equipment and make sure everything was secure. We decided to row ashore and walk across Jupiter Island to the Atlantic, ah, the *Atlantic ocean*, and play on the beach. I plan on sailing on that ocean soon.

The rest of the trip to Palm Beach went just as I had hoped it would. Ed and Trixie settled into a relaxing routine, and we all enjoyed each others company and the never before experience of this environment. Instead of being on the outside looking in...I'm on the inside looking out. I love the scenery.

Highlights of the Palm Beach experience include;

- Another successful overnight anchorage at Peanut Island without dragging.
- First trip out of the Lake Worth inlet under sail...genoa and main! Yes, the bilge light was on, and the water leak was back. Time to tell Ed I guess.
- The swooshing sound *Walkabout* made slicing through the 3-4 foot swells of the Atlantic, shooting spray over the fore-deck and we were thoroughly enjoying our romp in the Atlantic. Kind of like "damn the torpedoes, full speed ahead." Too much fun.
- Under sail through the inlet and back onto the waterway to begin our return trip north.

Ed was starting to wonder why I made so many trips below deck. "Well Ed, I didn't want to panic you, but we have a small leak in the bow, and we're taking on some water," I told him.

"WHAT THE FUCK ARE YOU TALKING ABOUT?!? YOU TELLING ME THIS SCOW IS SINKING??" *(UN-abbreviated sailor talk)* Ed asked in a not so polite tone.

"I'm not talking the Titanic here, just a little water."

I explained to him about the problem that we

found during our first outing and that it wasn't much to worry about if we took it easy. I tried to comfort him, "Don't worry Ed, you're not going to get your stinkin' Rolex wet!" Ed calmed down when I told him we were going to stop at a little bar on the waterway that had an accessible dock and that we could tie up to for beers and lunch. The bar was an enjoyable stopover, and it was about halfway to our planned overnight anchorage back at Peck Lake.

My pride and joy at anchor in Peck Lake.
Words can't describe the pride I am feeling.

Following a relaxing morning breakfast of mouth-watering bacon and eggs cooked up in the cozy galley, and many cups of coffee, we arrived back at Lowe's boatyard around mid-day. Our guests were going to be leaving early the next morning, so we all went out for a nice steak and lobster farewell dinner in town and reminisced about the highlights of our shakedown cruise.

Overall the entire trip with Ed and Trixie was terrific. Most everything we hoped to do we were able to do. So glad to share the excitement of our first voyage with them.

It was getting close to the time for us to think about heading home also. We were missing our families and critters and have a lot of plans to make about the future. An important and very serious consideration is whether two people can get along living in a space 37 feet by 12 feet for extended periods, and sometimes under very trying conditions...scary. Some of these trying conditions could be life or death situations.

Imagine what could happen if you are in a storm, and having a personal disagreement with your crew, and they choose not to follow orders! You won't have time for an argument here.

After a little more than a week on *Walkabout* and playing with our storage system, I came to the realization that there just wasn't enough storage, and there seemed to be a lot of wasted space behind bulkheads, cushions, etc. I met with David Lowe and Eric to go over the work that was needed to repair the leak, and also add the additional storage compartments along with some minor "punch list" items that the surveyor had recommended. They will call me with an estimate and get approval before starting work. I have found David, and his crew, a pleasure to work with.

We were each lost in our own thoughts during the trip home in a strange, settled, kind of way. Very reflective. We had a great time, and so far this seemed to fit us.

DECISION TIME IN THE ROCKY'S
25

We spent the summer sailing Destiny at the lake and enjoying our last days on her. The experience we had on *Walkabout* increased the fun and appreciation of the features Destiny had...just a smaller version of *Walkabout.* Nothing quite like having sex while anchored out.

Quite a bit of our time was spent selling property, horses, and "stuff." We were combining two households, and a lot of stuff had to go! Decisions had to be made to draft some fine folks to look after the remaining property and our smaller critters like dogs and cats. Kathy is going to quit her job...understandably that is very scary for her.

Kathy finally admitted she hadn't read her assigned books, as though I couldn't tell from our first trip. I had recommended *The Bluewater Handbook, How To Live Aboard A Boat, Sensible Cruising,* and *Chapman Piloting* just as necessary for starters, along with a few others, and always stressed how important I felt they were for her to get an understanding of what we were getting into.

A lot of people ask me if I were shipwrecked, and could only have one book, what would it be? I always say 'How to Build a Boat' - Stephen Wright

As for me? I am putting everything I have worked for into this adventure. We have planned for a max of two years commitment of time with a minimum of six to eight months to start with and then re-evaluate. We wanted to keep a good home base in Colorado with everything covered to minimize any problems.

Most of my relaxing time was spent reading about cruising in the islands and trying to understand and learn the tips from real life sailors. I was becoming a pretty competent sailor along the way, even if I have to say so myself. I love it!

I received the improvement and repair quotes from David Lowe and approved all the work to be done on *Walkabout*. We are planning to be back in Florida by mid- December so the work needed to be completed by then. They've got six months.

In addition to recording many dozens of music and VCR movie tapes, I spent a lot of time ordering more stuff that I found we needed to start cruising. There never seems to be an end to this, but it is a lot of fun reading about and trying to buy the right gear. So exciting!!

Some of the smaller items I could buy in Denver and then ship to Florida. For all the safety harnesses and lifelines, I purchased mountain climbing gear at REI. Really great stuff for safety. I ordered more charts and navigation supplies...our shipping boxes are starting to fill up and I'm thinking we may need even more storage compartments built into *Walkabout*.

I suddenly had the realization that a boat on the ocean needs to be a self-supporting little community...even if it's just for one person. A skipper needs to have a back-up plan for an almost endless possibility of problems. The lives of my crew and I depend on it. REALLY! It's to be expected to have to do some 'makeshift' repairs on a boat, so it's very imperative to have the necessary 'makeshift' kind of items available to jury rig almost any part that my boat might need. When we're off-shore, there won't be a store around to buy parts that may be needed.

Everything from engines, including an outboard, to rigging, to electrical and mechanical systems, and first aid, a sailor needs to have some type of plan for repair. Thank you, Dad, for teaching me how to 'fix stuff' and be creative.

I had an idea many years ago for a book to be called "Preparing For Failure." My friends always thought it sounded very pessimistic. I always looked at it as optimistic. The more prepared you are in case of a failure, the faster you can overcome it.

Now, I may get by without all this stuff, but in that case, I need to have a good abandon ship bag ready to go. No time to pack a bag while you're sinking.

A decent start for a basic abandon ship/emergency bag is; a good first aid kit, basic fishing essentials, rain gear, rubber repair kit, drinking water, plastic mirror, compass, basic tools (if you're a guy you'll know what that means), and power bars to eat.

In the future, I plan to add a waterproof handheld VHF radio, a waterproof GPS, and another EPIRB...and an updated book about how to build a boat. I'm sure there will be much more to add or delete, but I need to gain some experience to know what works and what doesn't. There is a limit to how much I can spend and still go on a walkabout.

I always loved being a Boy Scout in my younger days growing up in Missouri. I was fortunate enough to grow up in a small town outside of Kansas City with a lot of open country to explore and hike around in, complete with woods, streams, and lakes.

Almost every outing consisted of my Scout backpack loaded with all the necessary survival items I might need just in case of a nuke attack by the Russians since there wouldn't be a desk to hide under. Or, if I just needed to spend the afternoon daydreaming by a stream and doing kid stuff – my little metal canteen and metal mess kit, snake-bite kit, scout knife, raincoat, matches and a candy bar that I purchased with the pop bottle return money. It even included some string and safety pins in case I wanted to fish, oh, and band-aids and my big brother's copy of Playboy.

There's comfort in being self-sufficient.

As the summer and fall progressed, everything is falling into place. We planned on being back in Florida in mid-December to complete our move aboard *Walkabout*. A dozen large boxes were packed and sent to David Lowe's boatyard while we took a three-day train trip to Palm Beach. From there we rented a car and drove to Port Salerno.

We reserved bedroom suites on the Amtrak trains that made for some very memorable and romantic evenings. Great fun, and a terrific way to begin our adventure. We had some short stopovers in Chicago and Washington DC that allowed us to do a little exploring of those cities.

REPORTING FOR DUTY
26

It is overcast in mid-December when we drove into Port Salerno. The boxes that we shipped before leaving Denver had arrived just before we did. They appeared as though they were dropped in by a parachute that failed to open fully.

"I wonder what they would have looked like if you hadn't written "fragile" on them," Kathy said. "I hope it's not as bad as they look."

The competent crew at the boatyard had already moved *Walkabout* into a slip that allowed us to stay as long as needed to move aboard, and get our yacht ready for cruising.

I wanted to check some of the work that I had Lowe's do for me over the last few months, mainly because some of the work was to build-in several extra storage compartments into dead spaces between the interior walls/bulkheads and the hull. An amazing amount of space was wasted there. A lot of the gear that we sent would need to be put into that space from the beginning.

The extra compartments gave me almost 20% more storage, and they were needed. The storage system that I started back in May was modified to include the additional compartments.

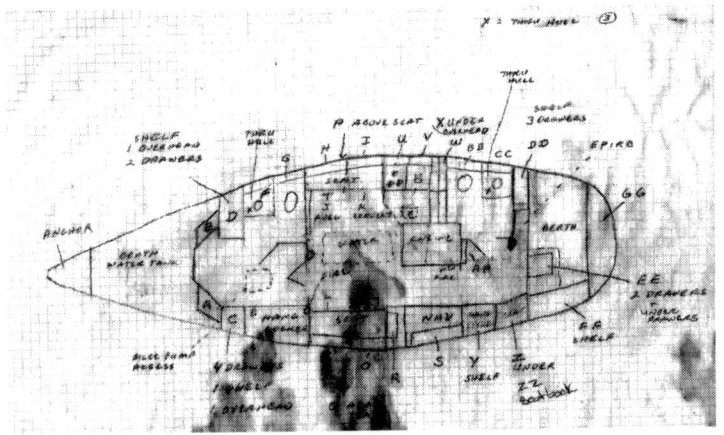

ITEM	QUANTITY	LOCATION
ACCENT	X0	I
ALKASELTZER	X1	AA
ALUMINUM FOIL	2	Z
ASHTRAY	1	Z
BACON CANNED	2	N
BACOS	1	GALLEY
BAGS SANDWICH	2	Z
BAGS TRASH	1	Z
BAKING POWDER	1	I
BEANS BAKED	1	N
BEANS BAKED LG	1	N
BEANS PORK & BEANS	6	ZZ
BEANS RANCH	1	N
BEANS REFRIED	1	ZZ
BISQUICK	1	X
BLEACH	X1	BB
BREADDING CORN	1	I
CAKE CHEESE JELLO	2	E
CAKE DEVILS FOOD	1	E
CAKE WHITE	2	E
CHEESE PARMESAN	1	I
CHILI NO BEANS	2	N
CHILI W/ BEANS	2	N
CHOCOLATE HOT COCO	1	GALLEY
CLEANER SOFT SCRUB	X0	EE
CLEANER, BIO-T	1	
CLEANER, LYSOL	1	
CLEANER, MULTI-PURPOSE	1	GG
CLEANER, WOOLITE	2	BB
COCOA	1	I

FOOD STORES

The above example is an actual printout of part of our food stores. There are many hundreds of items in several categories, and dozens of locations.

Every item, including nuts, bolts, and washers on *Walkabout,* was inventoried and entered into my computer. Everything could then be sorted by item, quantity, and/or location, so it was easy to generate a shopping list for re-provisioning. Anything we needed, we knew if we had it, and we knew the exact location to find it. This is a fantastic time-saver. It required many hours to set up, but it is easy to maintain after that. It is a very fun way to spend the day!

Anal? Maybe, but I'll know when I need more Ruffles chips or to restock more 1/4-20 stainless nuts.

We quickly settled into working on the boat and enjoying our quiet evenings together while planning our first trip. Our initial plans were to circumnavigate Florida heading down to the Keys and then up the West coast to Fort Myers. From there we could navigate to Lake Okeechobee and back to Port Salerno. Yes, it is possible with a shoal draft boat. Worst case, we would just spend the winter in the Keys.

I figured it would take us the rest of the winter, and give us lots of experience on the boat...relatively safely. If we got into trouble, there would always be help close by. **God bless the United States Coast Guard!**

An additional benefit would be that friends could fly down and cruise with us for a while without leaving the country.

We met an interesting Canadian couple working on their gorgeous 44-foot cutter rigged sailboat, Wavedancer. Wavedancer is always stored at Lowe's for the summer, and they come down every winter and cruise to the Bahamas. We met several other cruisers that do the same thing every winter just like the Erickson's have done. Such an interesting group of sailors.

Dieter is originally from Germany and is a real estate developer now living in Toronto. We are about the same age and physical size. Rosemary, his long term companion, is smaller and a little younger than Kathy but they hit it off from the start.

Everyone in the marina was surprised that we had become friends with Dieter since he mostly kept to himself. They all said we couldn't learn from a more experienced sailor, and we should take advantage of his knowledge if he offered it.

Kathy and I enjoyed so many pleasant evenings with them, having dinner or playing cards, it was all fun. We are becoming close friends.

Kathy loved introducing them to her famous Sloppy Joe sandwich. That became one of Dieter's favorite meals along with chicken fried steak with mashed potatoes and gravy.

We explained our plans but, with encouragement from Rosemary, I was getting pressured by my crew to go with them to the Bahamas. I gotta say it was becoming very tempting. We could learn from one of the best sailing couples in the marina for free! I just wasn't confident enough of my sailing skills to take on such a trip. I am putting together quite a nice abandon ship bag, so that's a comfort.

We threw out a wide net fishing for knowledge about actually sailing in the Bahamas, and harvested a great deal of information from Dieter. Things such as proper protocol in the islands. How well does loran work over there? Pirates...are they real? (Yes they are!) How do we legally carry firearms or other protective items onboard? Any certain islands or areas to be aware of? Of course, these questions prompted them to share some fun stories.

To make the passage to the Bahamas, we need to cross the famous Gulf Stream. This powerful ocean river is about 45 miles wide, out of the approximately 65-mile width of the Florida Straight, and flows north at about 2.5 knots or more. If there happens to be a northern wind, it can make for some very exciting sea conditions.

The Bahama islands themselves are very unique cruising grounds. We are very fortunate to have them right outside our door. Most of the islands are cays, pronounced keys, are low in elevation with the highest being around 200 feet, and an average in height in the high teens. There are approximately 700 islands in over 1000 square miles that make up the Bahamas. Flat islands that have been formed by coral. Pretty boring vegetation however.

The Bahamas have some of the clearest water in the world. One can see down 30 or more feet in most areas. The average temperature in the winter is 77°...I think I can handle that!

While crossing the Gulf Stream, we will be going over a part of the ocean that is 10,000 feet deep, my depth finder doesn't have that many numbers, and when we get to the Bahama Bank it will average 10-30 feet in the island chains...ah, that's better.

We listened to all of their stories. "It's much safer to travel in groups," Dieter said. They told us about island hopping and running across other boats that they had met a few islands ago, and that the number of encounters would grow as they progressed thru the islands. Casual beach picnics or cockpit cocktails with other crews were always going on...or not, your choice. Real *Fantasy Island* kind of stuff.

This is the kind of stuff I imagined the sailing life would be like. I would lean back and close my eyes, while anchored out on Destiny on Chatfield Lake and let my imagination take over.

Kathy was sold on the idea, and that surprised me. "We can do this, I know we can. They can teach us so much, and come on...we're talking about the Bahamas sweetheart," she whispered in my ear one very romantic evening.

"How close are you to reading all the material I gave you? This is important stuff! When are they planning on heading out?" I asked her the next morning.

"I'm working on it skipper, and will have the homework finished by the time we leave," she said.

I guess we will be leaving in mid-January...I'm still not 100% sold on this, but the temptation for the adventure and challenge is getting to be too much.

Dieter finished his work getting Wavedancer ship-shape for spending the winter in the Bahamas, and so did we with *Walkabout*.

Dieter, and some of the Lowes dock crew, gave me proper instructions on how to sand the teak rails and brightwork and apply a new coat or two of spar varnish. It came out great! Surprise...this should be done every six months but worth it.

I figure we are as ready as we'll ever be. One of

the last items we needed was an outboard motor for Crawlabout, and I was able to get a deal on a used one that seemed to fit our need. Another luxury item we allowed ourselves were a pair of stainless folding bicycles to get around while on shore. They fit perfectly in the inflatable so they would be easy to take ashore for our land-side excursions.

We are so proud of our pristine yacht. Crawlabout is securely lashed down on the fore-deck. Our outboard and two folding bikes aft. Secure for the crossing.

STARTING OUT
27

"When the draft of your vessel exceeds the depth of the water, you are most assuredly, aground."- Ian Walsh

January 17th '92; our small fleet departed the marina under power around 11:00 am. and headed out to the Inter-coastal to start our trip to Palm Beach. There, we would spend the night before heading East to the islands. The thrill of it all...the butterflies in my stomach were giving me an anxiety attack. This is the real thing now!

We had no sooner rounded the point and onto the inter-coastal when Wavedancer ran aground. Wavedancer has a draft of 8 feet and the shoaling, that this part of the waterway is famous for, reared its ugly head. Dieter tried everything to free Wavedancer, but she was well stuck in the muck.

After discussing the problem on the radio, we came up with a plan to bring *Walkabout* close to Wavedancer and toss a line. Dieter would then tie the line to his main halyard while Kathy tied our end off to a cleat on our stern. I then eased *Walkabout* into forward gear, and gently pulled Wavedancer to port-side acting much like a fulcrum, which in turn raised the depth of his keel and got her freed. I continued to pull Wavedancer sideways to the center of the channel with greater depth.

Shortly after resuming our trip Wavedancer was aground for a second time but not as bad. This time, we threw a line to their stern, and I pulled them back into deeper water. *"OK Dieter, time to start watching your depth gauge a little closer,"* I quietly say to myself.

It was decided that *Walkabout* would then lead the way due to our shallower draft and I could alert Dieter early if it started shoaling up shallower than his eight feet.

The remainder of the trip to Palm Beach was very relaxing, including a three- hour layover due to a broken bridge at Hobe Sound. We just dropped anchor in the waterway and kicked back until the bridge was repaired.

Our little fleet docked at Riviera Beach Marina in Palm Beach for the evening so we could cast off early the next morning. It would be a short trip out to the inlet. We had a brief "Captains" meeting with cocktails aboard Wavedancer this evening to go over our finale plans for departure. Anxiety had started to set in again for the crew of *Walkabout* as we tried to settle in for the evening. Tomorrow was going to be a huge day for us as far as taking the next step to really going cruising. Of course, we'll have the comfort of Dieter and Rosemary close by. They are the deciding factor for me even to make this trip.

OUT THE INLET
28

"Jan 18, '92 7:55 am;

Lovely clear day with north wind 3-5 knots." Kathy notes in the ships off-shore log; *"OFF WE GO!!! Into the rising sun."*

WOW! The salt air, the gentle breeze in our faces, a calm Atlantic, and under full sail...how can it get better?!?

Taken from Wavedancer
Three sheets to the wind!

Wavedancer early in the trip.

Everything is working as it should. The crew performed like a well-oiled machine, and we are really enjoying the experience. By 10 am the wind has shifted to the northeast and increased to 14 knots. By 11 am the wind continued to shift to more southeast.

We plan to sail straight thru to Nassau, Bahamas. Dieter needs to be there by a specific date, so we have it planned to get there a few days early, re-provision, and get in some sightseeing.

"The lovely thing about cruising is that planning usually turns out to be of little use."- Dom Degnon

Five pm; 26° 26' 64 N, 79° 20' 56 W.

During our radio communications with Wavedancer, it is determined that with the wind shift our headway was not as good as it should be. So, it was decided we should motor-sail to maintain our desired course and speed. We furled in the genoa and lowered the mizzen and fired up 'ol Carl Perkins to assist the main. *Walkabout* can't run as close to the wind as Wavedancer does but with the assist of Carl, we could maintain close to the same speed and course. I had to run Carl pretty hard.

I took advantage of this time to practice the art of 'dead reckoning' to plot our location on my chart and compare my findings to our Loran. I soon realize that Loran readings, for the most part, are just close guesses and are affected by a lot of different things, especially in the islands. I continued to compare my readings with Wavedancer since they have a GPS. At this point, my dead reckoning is off but closer to our actual position than the Loran. Oh, that's swell!

Speaking of swell, they were getting larger now and coming from the east. So, now we are close hauled and heading more into the waves.

We are having to wear our life vests and safety harnesses full time...even when going below. Damn, now I can't see her perfect nipples through her damp t-shirt.

I wasn't thrilled with the constant hum of the diesel, but we are maintaining a good course and speed. Overall, It has been a very enjoyable cruise...until now. It now seems that 'ol Carl was running rough and we are losing speed and RPM.

"Why am I smelling diesel?" I inquired to Kathy. "Do you smell that? It can't be exhaust fumes since we are heading more into the wind."

As I went below to plot our dead recon position, the diesel smell is stronger than in the cockpit! What the hell? I noticed the bilge light had come on a little earlier, but shut off after a few seconds, so I didn't think much about it. I checked the bilge and saw some water sloshing around that had a film on top. That film turned out to be diesel fuel.

(More sailor talk here)

"What the fuck is going on now?!"

Kathy heard me all the way up in the cockpit.

"What's going on down there skipper? Are you OK?"

"We are leaking diesel somehow, somewhere! I need to check the engine compartment."

The seas were building along with an increase in the wind. It is getting harder to keep up the pace of Wavedancer, more so now with the misfirings of the diesel.

I checked on Kathy to make sure she was holding course since the auto-helm could not handle the waves, and shifting wind, so it needed to be turned off, and she had to steer by hand. Welcome to becoming a real sailor! Now, I have to let her know I'll be below for a while, "only call me if it's an emergency." She's not a happy crew right now.

I removed the access hatch to the engine compartment and could see a stream of fuel coming from an injector tube. I proceed to expel every cuss-word known to man along with several that I just made up. I contacted Dieter on the VHF and described the problem as I see it. "Not good," came his reply. "Do you have a spare tube in your engine kit? If you do, it will need to be changed."

I was so proud of my engine kit. I did a complete inventory of the items and confirmed the contents with several friends, including Dieter. "Looks like everything you might need including filters and belts," was the consensus from all.

I had Kathy turn off the engine, and that meant we had to alter our course, and sail close-hauled as best we could to maintain any speed at all. I could tell Dieter was not happy, at this point, after I explained our situation to him, and he was also getting a little testy with the building weather.

I identified the leaking tube and removed it. This is turning into a real challenge, working almost up-side-down, in a building sea, combined with the stink of the fuel mixing with sea water. Bilges aren't known for pleasant smells to start with.

I'm glad Kathy and I are both wearing our Sea-Bands...they seem to be working. She's hanging in there OK.

Since the Perkins is a four-cylinder engine, there are four injector tubes in the kit. Perfect! "Well...son-of-a-bitch!!" OK, how fucking stupid am I? I had no idea that the tubes were all different shapes. Each tube had it's own shape depending on the cylinder it fed. I hadn't noticed that two of the tubes were exactly the same.

As luck would have it, the only tube I didn't have was the one that was leaking. In trying to bend one of the tubes to match the bad one, it cracked. I tried several times to stop the leak with tape only to be met with very high pressure that just blew thru the tape. I knew it was futile...but I had to try. Dieter laughed at that.

Now, after several hours of delay, I contacted Wavedancer and explained our situation. Not good news. Dieter said they would have to leave us and continue on their way to Nassau. He gave me the latitude and longitude and compass heading for Freeport, Grand Bahama and told us we should head there for repairs. "WTF?? Leave us out here?" I said. He replied, "Sorry, but we have to go."

"Let me make sure I have this right. Two rookies, on a broken ship, with a building storm, a 'close guess' loran, it's starting to get dark, and we are going to be abandoned? REALLY!! I would have been in the Keys by now if I had my way," saying in a light way and still try to make a point.

"That's the best we can do. I have an important meeting I need to keep in Nassau," came his reply. "Good luck, and let us know when you reach Nassau. Don't try to enter Freeport in the dark. Wait until morning. You'll be fine."

*If you can not arrive in daylight, then stand off
well clear, and wait until dawn.-Tristan Jones*

I explained our situation to Kathy, and she was
not happy either...and, she is now getting scared. She
heard what was said on the radio. All of a sudden it is
now my fault! I should have known about the tubes. I
really think if there were any way she could get
aboard Wavedancer she would.

We lost radio contact with Wavedancer shortly
after their masthead light disappeared over the
horizon...we are now alone.

STRANDED ON THE HIGH SEAS
29

"Sail 73° NE to 26°28' 30 N 78°46' 00 W. Hang off-shore at least 4 miles." Yeah, right!

Well...there go my hopes of erotic sex on the high seas tonight.

With our change in course, we can use more sail and not run the Perkins as often to maintain progress. But, since it has gotten dark, we'll need the running lights, the radar uses a lot of battery power, and I definitely will need it in the dark. We will only run the Perkins often enough to keep the batteries charged. The refrigerator uses quite a bit of juice too.

Another thing...the auto-helm doesn't work very well in the rough seas, and it also uses a lot of power. We had to steer by hand constantly. I'm open to any good news anytime now!!

By 11:00 pm we could see the lights of Freeport. The winds have increased to 18-20 knots and still coming from the SE. In the darkness of the black sea, some of the waves have turned into whitecaps, my mind is seeing them as hundreds of glittering icebergs. They are now crashing over our bow.

Kathy hasn't taken her head out of the bucket I put in the cockpit for her. I feel very bad for her...she's really trying to help. Sea-Bands only work so well for so long. I gotta say that considering what we are going thru, they worked great!

After many hours at the helm, my weary mind called upon a past event for some advice. As Captain and her friend, I feel responsible for this.

There are many events in life that can create fear. Girls, first sex, getting married, having a kid, answering a fire call, starting a new business, divorce...just to name a few.

The most scared situation I ever faced, until now, happened while camping out in the Colorado mountains. I was going through a tough personal time and was trying to figure out what I wanted to be when I grow up.

Dutch, my favorite horse, and I decided we would like to go camping...away from everyone. Fuck everything...I'm gonna go hide out for a while. I chose the Arapaho National Forest for its beauty and remote location.

It was a beautiful day, and we rode for several hours into the back-country without seeing another person. As we came upon a large colorful meadow I decided would be a perfect location to make camp for the evening, so we did. After gathering some rocks, I made a small campfire and settled into a reflective evening enjoying one of our famous Colorado sunsets.

As the evening progressed, we settled in for the night, it was so quiet, peaceful...not a sound anywhere. Millions of diamonds on the black velvet sky...a million dollar view. All of a sudden it hit me...we are miles from anywhere and totally alone. Mountain lions and bears live here! I am stuck, and no idea how to get out. Fear set in...what can I do? I had to conquer the fear...I had no other choice! I have not been afraid since. A wonderful experience! Loved that horse.

Ships log: *I think that it is about this time we are*

both realizing just how serious our situation is. People die doing this kind of stuff if they make the wrong decisions while not quite knowing what to do...correct decisions need to be made, and fast. Kathy's faith in her "skipper" is fading fast also.

I thank God for our radar. It is like a crystal ball of sorts. It can see your future. Is there something out there you are about to hit unless changes are made? Yes, there is!

I had been tracking a blip on the radar screen, and every reading indicated we were going to collide. With Kathy's deteriorated condition I wasn't able to spend much time below at the radar, so by the time I could see the ship's lights we were committed to our course for the best chance of making it. We were running with a reefed main only while fighting the waves and wind. I could now see the lights of what appeared to be a huge football stadium bearing down on our starboard side...fast.

I had to start up the Perkins to assist the main in an effort to beat that large ship past the collision point. It was very tense as that towering ship, and our little boat got closer...we could see it now, pushing a good sized bow wave...a large tanker with the lights of a small town...we could hear it now too! I had the crippled engine pushed to its max.

"GOOD SIZED BOW WAVE..." I shouted, "coming about hard to starboard." We took the bow wave head-on. I gained a new respect for those jerks.

It seems every container ship and cruise ship in the Atlantic is intent on running us down. I soon became pretty good at tracking their course and speed, and I am amazed at how often we are on a "collision course" with them. Seems like most of them don't respond to radio calls either. "Hey!! we're under sail here, and we have the right-of-way!" I kept saying to myself. I'm sure they know that but are smiling while saying "fuck you shit head," to themselves, and continue to head straight for us.

We were sailing under a reefed main back and forth 4 to 5 miles off Grand Bahama, in 4-5 foot waves, and will be for the next 6 hours until daylight. I gotta say I am getting a little scared at this point. I had faced danger when I was on the fire department, but that danger only lasted for minutes...this is continuing for hours and still no end in sight. I will still have to get into some strange port in these rough seas when daylight comes.

The sweet looks that I used to get from my first mate, Kathy, that would say to me "you got me into this sweetheart, thank you," have turned into "you got me into this asshole, now get me out." Hey, I wanted to go to the keys, remember?

My main concern is I have to do everything I can to keep Kathy safe. Her safety is most important to me.

"Being hove to in a long gale is the most boring way of being terrified I know."- Donald Hamilton

Taking the time to read The Bahamas Cruising Guide book, it is advised not to enter Freeport...it is very commercial and not cruiser friendly. The next best port will be Xanadu and Bahamia Bay.

Bahamia Bay has a marina, although not a full-service marina, as well as the resort that should allow us some relief after this trauma we're going through. The entrance, listed as tricky, should be pretty straight forward. The channel is very narrow with reefs on both sides, and only about six feet of water at low tide. The only landmark is the tall Xanadu Hotel, and we need to keep a close eye on the reefs.

In retrospect, I should have given more thought to heading back to Palm Beach for the repairs since I was familiar with that inlet. I could have also been sure of getting the parts needed for repairs there also.

After a very harrowing night, the welcoming glow of the early morning daylight smiled on our weary bodies. Kathy was doing a little better, but mainly because she had nothing left to put in the bucket. I have been up for over twenty-four hours, and I don't think she had much sleep either. Neither one of us has eaten in the last 24 hours.

Is the name change curse real??

After getting close to the proper coordinates, we spotted the large hotel that marked the Xanadu Resort and Bahamia Bay. Now, we need to locate the outer marker for the channel through the reef. To continue the curse of this "baptismal" cruise, to enter the outer channel *Walkabout* would be exposed to a following sea with 3-5 foot swells.

I don't know who named them swells cause they're not!

As near as I could understand about the designed hull speed of this Irwin, it is about six knots. After entering the channel, I realized that the fucking swell speeds were almost exceeding that.

All sail was dropped, and we are running hard with a crippled Perkins, and the swells were trying their damnedest to broach *Walkabout*, and, and, and..."God, will this never end?" All the while injecting a lot of diesel fuel into the bilge that will have to be dealt with. I had to shut bilge the pump off before entering the channel.

This channel appears to be only about forty feet

wide, and it's all I can do to keep her in a relatively straight line. The only good thing is it's not at low tide. It seems like a lifetime of sheer terror for us.

I'm sure some of the problems are due to my inexperience in these conditions and with my limited sailing time on *Walkabout*. Fact remains, these are the real problems we are facing.

Kathy is on reef watch, but still very seasick. She's a real trooper. I wish she would quit calling me General Custer however.

A SAIL ABOARD WALKABOUT

LANDFALL GRAND BAHAMA
30

We limped our crippled ship into the bay around eight am. It and we are a mess. Our once proud and pristine little yacht stunk so bad with diesel fuel we couldn't spend much time below deck. Several pieces of gear decided not to stay in their assigned locations, so they were strewn about...there's a lot of work to be done down here. I think something heavy fell on my Ruffles, damn it!

We are lucky checking into the marina mainly because of the dock-master, Jake. Even with all of the problems getting here, we are excited about meeting our first resident of the Bahamas. He was middle-aged, about 5'9" with a stocky build and a friendly smile. We explained our problem with the diesel fuel, and he picked out a perfect slip.

We were instructed to run up a yellow quarantine flag until cleared by customs.

We filled out the paperwork and contacted the local customs office to check us in and told us they would be out here in a few hours. Jake showed us the slip he has chosen, and it is perfect. It is directly behind the Xanadu resort kitchen...open grease pit and all.

Jake explained, "You can pump out your bilge into buckets and dump them into the grease pit. I even have some buckets you can use. You can use my phone to call a local marine mechanic." This guy is a real "Godsend" for us. Our pathetic looks and smell helped also.

Jake recommended and called a mechanic friend of his, and he said he would be out after lunch to check out our problem.

The crew finally had a chance to sit in the cockpit, take some deserved deep breaths, and relax, even for just a few minutes. We looked around and revered in the realization we were in a foreign country, we got here by boat, and we were still alive!

Reality set back in after a few minutes, damn it. We looked at the work that needed to be done before we could even think about spending the night below...and it had to be done now.

"OK, here's our plan of attack. We get Crawlabout off the deck and alongside *Walkabout.* I'll hold the buckets so as the catch the water pumped out of the bilge while you turn the pump on and off. Once these buckets are filled, I'll push back to the dock, and then we will dump the buckets into the grease pit. And repeat. Got it?"

I really wish I could take a picture of the look on her face. It's the kind you blow up or throw darts at.

"Are you fucking kidding me? I need some sleep!" she asked and demanded.

I replied, "Here's the best part...after we do it the first time we get to do it again with soap and water. I need to pull up all the access panels so we can wash out the bilge."

Kathy was too stunned to reply, the looks she gave me said it all. Sadly, she knew I was right.

"We can't really start with the pumping until we clear with customs because we can't give him any idea about what's going on. I'm sure he would classify us as an environmental disaster, and impound our boat."

All passports and boat papers are in order, so we cleared the port of entry just fine. Guns were properly locked up, and we weren't smuggling drugs. Great! We get to run up the Bahamian courtesy flag! Yeah!!!

As soon as he left, we started to work in earnest.

I can't guess how many buckets it took to empty the bilge twice...all's I can say is it was a hell of a lot. The kitchen staff had given us some grease soap that they use on their dishes, to help break down the diesel, and that got things pretty clean. These folks are great!

Only during brief breaks could we take any time and really try to enjoy our colorful surroundings. I know we both felt some disappointment in the last twenty-four hours, but "it is what it is" as the saying goes. We made it.

Jake's mechanic friend, Perry, came by and knew exactly what to order if he couldn't find one on the island. I asked him to order two. One for a spare. He said it could take a day or two and would let Jake know. Another great guy.

As darkness approached, *Walkabout* is finally getting back to ship-shape condition. "I think we should be able to sleep in a real bed below tonight," I announced. "We'll still need to leave all of the access hatches open to dry out the bilge." Ah...the sweet smell of bleach.

The crew of *Walkabout is* basically the walking dead at this point. In the last forty hours, we have gone through the excitement of leaving Florida, the ugly diesel problem, and the constant, energy draining, pounding of a rough sea, **and** in the dark.

No sex again tonight.

"Do you think it will get better from here?" Kathy inquired as she snuggled up.

"I don't think it will get any worse. If we could make it through this past forty hours we can make it through anything," I said with cocky confidence.

What a glorious morning it is! Amazing what a good nights sleep can do! Breakfast and coffee in the cockpit and being proud of all the work we did yesterday. It is going to be a very pleasant and mostly sunny day.

Since we had to wait on the parts for the fuel repair, we are going to try out our folding bikes, and pedal into Freeport for the day. One of the exciting things for us is to enjoy the experience of being in another country. The only other times we had been out of the good 'ol USA was some short trips to Mexico and the British Virgins sailing.

These bikes are so cool to have. We start out for the short trip into Freeport and *"holy crap Batman...they are trying to run us down even here. I had thought it was only the big ships, but it's the cars also!"*

"They drive on the left here ya know," Kathy said with a smile. Jeez...who would've thought?

Thrilling to navigate a "roundabout" here...kind of a death trap as I see it.

Freeport is the second largest city in the Bahamas and has a "tourist trap" kind of feel because of all the tourist type of shops. For the most part, it seemed pretty run down. It has a Mexican border town kind of look with an island flare. Lots of bright colors on old buildings that could use a good coat of paint. Interesting stuff and fun to poke around. We rather enjoyed the atmosphere and the people.

It is reported that they had a little snow in January of '77.

We were introduced to some delicious Bahamian style conch fritters and beers for lunch at a local restaurant and thoroughly enjoyed our outing. A nice relief from the pounding of the boat ride the past few days.

Arriving back at the marina, Perry was working on our fuel problem. Perry was able to get the parts locally and was almost finished installing the injector tube when we arrived. He was able to get me a spare also.

"We are almost back in business," Kathy said.

We poured ourselves some wine and kicked back in our favorite spot...the cockpit. I'm happy that *Walkabout* has handled the way she has. Seems to be pretty forgiving. I started out loving her, and now I respect her.

"The goal is not to sail the boat, but rather to help the boat sail herself."- John Rousmaniere

"We'll look for a good weather window to set sail for Nassau if you're willing to continue. What do you think?" I asked.

"We're almost halfway there, so let's give it a shot. Besides, I think Dieter and Rosemary will be waiting for us," Kathy responded.

I thought about it and added, "I'm still

disappointed with them for leaving us. On the one hand, it's nice to think Dieter has that much faith in my boat handling skills, but on the other hand, I'm not so sure of those skills myself. We were in some tough shit out there Kathy, and at times I didn't know what to do...I didn't want to let you down either. We're not at Chatfield sweetheart. The best way to get back at them is to prove that Dieter is right," I laughed as I thought about the events of the last few weeks.

"It has been exciting even if not always fun at times," I added. I'm so proud of you."

We decided we would spend tomorrow morning to finish getting *Walkabout* ready to cast off. We'll take a short trip of a few miles up the coast to Port Lucaya and in through the Bell Channel to anchor for the night. That gives us a chance to test the Perkins and check everything else after our pounding.

Bell Channel and Port Lucaya are where we *wanted* to go the first night, but we were closer to Bahamia Bay. We were too drained to try for Port Lucaya even though it is supposed to be an easier approach.

It was a nice trip from Bahamia Bay, even with high waves and a brisk wind. Once inside, it was an easy anchor with many other cruisers nearby. Most had come in to get out of the storms.

Ships log: With each new day and challenge, we are gaining more confidence in our seamanship abilities. Here we are, anchored in this harbor with real-life cruisers, and starting to feel like we are fitting in. These are the people that I have read about and admired over the years. As I look around at the other boats, I wonder what kind of exciting tales they have about their adventures.

Retiring to the cockpit has now become a ritual

for us. Glasses of wine and broken Ruffles chips and reflection about our challenges for the day. Now regretting our giving up smoking.

There are long, ongoing discussions about our next step for this adventure. The weather forecast for the next week or so is not ideal for sailing. We have been thru quite a bit up to now and survived, so that gave us some false encouragement. There will be a short window starting tomorrow when the storms shouldn't be as severe.

"Do we chance it or not?" Kathy asked.

"It's 60 miles to Great Stirrup Cay at the top of the Berry Islands. Should take about ten hours if we're lucky. It has decent anchorages in either Bertram Cove or Panton Cove, so we could anchor there and check on the weather as we go," I said.

Other sailors told me this was unusually bad weather right now. Somewhere along the line, I must have pissed-off Davy Jones.

Later on, during our relaxing evening, I whispered in Kathy's ear, "Listen swab, I want to see you naked in the Captains cabin tonight so me can have me way with you, eh wench."

"Aye, aye Captain," came the smiling reply.

My first mates' perky nipples were starting to show through her t-shirt as our passion for the evening began to build. It's a beautiful night with the stars and wavy glow of the shore lights dancing on the water. We are seasoned sailors now and are going to enjoy our little slice of heaven, on the high seas, on our mini-yacht, and in a foreign country. Our surroundings looked just like a scene in a movie.

Directly above the master state-room bed is a hatch that opens above to the aft deck. Slowly undressing each other in the soft glow of the harbor lights shining thru the cabin portals, some long passionate kisses, and the arousing full contact of our naked bodies we rewarded ourselves with a benefit of our situation.

4:30 am;

Up early and took a hike around the deck to check our holding and gear. Satisfied, I went below to make coffee and check the weather reports. Kathy smelled the coffee and made her way into the cockpit..."nice glow ya got." We would sure like to get an early start making our way to Nassau today if possible.

We should be able to make the 60 miles to Great Stirrup Cay in the Berry Islands, in 10-11 hours with fair conditions. The forecast is for a mostly clear day with winds from the S.E. 15-20. Plus or minus three ft waves. Not perfect but going to get worse in a few days.

With our renewed energy and optimism, we raised anchor and said goodbye to Port Lucaya. Cleared the channel at 0600 and set course to 25° 33' 30 N 077° 42' 30 W by steering 141° at the start, and adjusting our course many times along the way.

Kathy's Quote from ships log; "06:00 Leaving Port Lucaya. Dark and rough outside. Almost turned back but we want to get to Nassau. Forecast not good for later on if we stay. Nervous trip."

This entry made me feel sad for her, and at the same time, I am so proud of her for hanging in here right now.

We are running with the full main only because the winds have increased along with the wave heights.

Matt Helm, the autopilot, just doesn't work very well in rough seas...damn it!

All things considered, the trip went OK. Kathy did manage to squeeze in a little time to catch up on some of the information that I asked her to read a year ago. She couldn't have absorbed much, I could tell because every time a wave hit us, and that is getting more constant as we progress, she would raise her head to see if we are going down...no doubt to get a head start toward the life raft.

GREAT STIRRUP CAY
31

As we approached Great Stirrup in the area off Bertram Cove, we could see a large cruise ship anchored in the cove entrance. I knew this was a popular anchorage for cruise ships but felt it was worth a shot. With the wind coming out of the northeast, it would only be an acceptable anchorage at best, and there didn't seem to be a lot of room.

A few miles further to the east, and then around to the south side, in the lee of the island, and into Panton Cove became a more attractive option. Wind 20-22 MPH. Another hour or two of getting the shit beat out of us was all.

I just now noticed we no longer have our stern anchor. That explains that sound I heard a bit ago. "FUCK!!"

"We're down to two anchors...this is not good!" I exclaimed.

"The sea will show you everything you did wrong."

As we continued east, the waves and winds are relentless on us. This is becoming a storm pretty fast. It's taking everything I have just to control *Walkabout* to make it as comfortable as possible. Kathy had become of no help with the steering or operation of the boat, so her only duty is to read the island navigation directions to enter Panton Cove and to not throw up in the cockpit. We have to get in there before this crap gets any worse. The only other choice is to hang out offshore until morning, and after what we went thru at Grand Bahama that was not an attractive option.

Really!! We can not go thru that again after this long hard sail.

"Steer for that gap between the two islands to the southeast," Kathy directed. "After we get past the east end of the first island steer south."

"Kathy, that 'gap,' as you call it, appears to be only about 100 feet wide, the east most island seems to be just a very large rock," I said. "I don't think we can make it. Are you sure?"

"Yes, damn it! Don't you think I can read?"

With the main dropped, the swing keel raised, and running on the Perkins, we shot for the 'gap.' I was wrong...it wasn't barely even fifty feet wide.

"Reread it again damn it...once we start in there, there is no turning back." I am getting really scared at this point...and I don't scare all that easy.

The closer we got to the gap, the waves turned into breakers. No shit! We are only about 25 to 30 feet offshore, and it's getting very shallow.

"Kathy...are you sure about this??" And with that, she threw the book at me.

I have the Perkins at about half throttle as we started thru the 'gap' in the islands, and it is a very harrowing experience. Constantly fighting the waves coming from our stern that keep pushing us. We are basically a 37 ft diesel-powered surfboard. My adrenaline is running over the top.

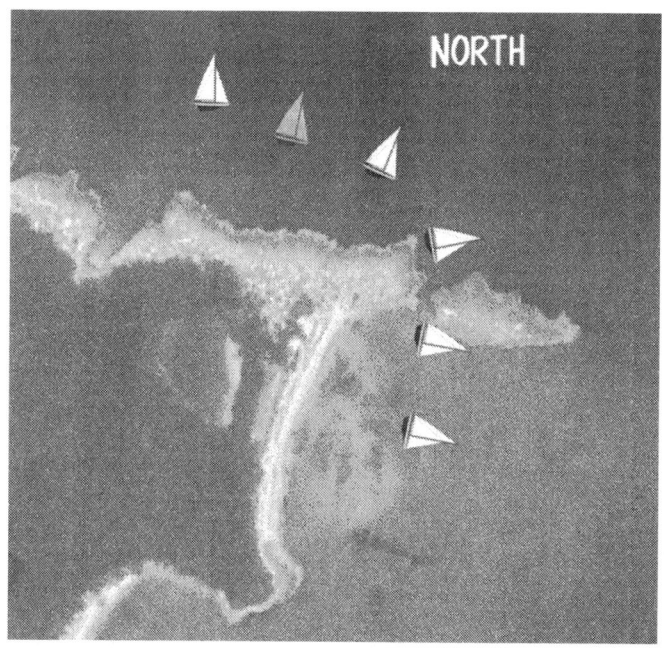

This has to rank as one of the dumbest things a sailor has done. You're never too old to learn something stupid.

As we went thru the gap, there is a beach directly on the starboard and less than 20 feet away. At the bottom of a wave, *Walkabout* actually hit the bottom of the ocean. I had to go to full throttle and hard to port to stay off the beach and try to power thru the waves into open water. **"WHAT THE FUCK IS GOING ON? GET OFF MY FUCKING BACK!"** I screamed to the world at the top of my lungs.

We are what seemed like inches away from serious injury or death, or at the very least...the loss of the boat.

Once we got back into more open water, I grabbed the guide book to read those directions. Kathy had us going into the wrong island. The proper island and directions warned about the east approach to Panton Cove. Of course, the gap was the totally wrong way to go and very dangerous. I had to really contain my anger because she is having a rough time as it is, and I couldn't afford to have a mutiny on my hands. I need her!! She *is* doing the best she can under some very difficult conditions, and I know that.

As Captain of this ship, it is my fault, and I accept that responsibility. I should have taken more caution and read the directions myself. We are so lucky to still be in one piece and almost dry. *Walkabout* performed perfectly. I sure hope no one saw that.

As our nerves settled down, we continued to motor in the direction of the anchorage. I shouldn't have been surprised to see it already crowded with other boats seeking shelter from the mounting storm. Some have been here for days. The cove is shallow for the most part, maybe a little over six feet in some areas. Choices to drop anchor are extremely limited. Much calmer water here. Since I didn't want to get too close to the boats that were already anchored, I chose to try an open expanse of water to the west of the other boats, soon to discover why the area is open.

We both knew that the moment we arrived in the 'arena' that we were this afternoons entertainment for the other crews. We were in such bad emotional and physical shape we weren't concerned about how good we look...survival mode has kicked in. Let the show begin.

We ran aground as soon as we started entering the cove in the soft bottom...*of course we did!!*...I found the bottom of this ocean, again!! This is one fucking test after another. None of this shit appeared in my dreams. We are stuck and unable to back out. No offers of help came over the radio. A plan was developed...we have to unleash Crawlabout and use the main halyard to lower it over the side.

Our plan, at this point, is to carry the stern Danforth anchor and rode using the dingy off the stern of *Walkabout* toward deeper water. Oh! Wait! We lost that anchor getting in here! Backup plan...we have to use the bow Danforth and row it out as far as I can, drop the anchor and use a cockpit wench to kedge us to the rear as the Perkins idled in reverse. The plan works perfectly, thanks to Kathy. We needed to back out as straight as possible. Teamwork on display.

OK, we're out of the fire and into the safety of the boiling pot. We still need to find another spot to anchor, and it's getting late. We're tired, hungry, and our nerves are shot after the grueling sail. I haven't seen a smile from the crew in many hours.

There appears to be enough room between the other boats and the south shore of the island, so we headed in that direction. We are on the lee side of the island with an offshore breeze that would work well for us, and still leave decent swing room for everyone.

A significant fear and concern for all boaters is that you get a good anchorage for your boat, and someone will come in and encroach on your territory. That comforting "swing room" that you had before is now compromised. I really had no other choice, and everyone is very understanding. We're all in the same boat, so to speak.

We had already given the other boat crews something to laugh about during their cocktail hour, so therefore we paid for our admission.

Ah...anchored at last. Since there is only about six feet of water under us at most, we didn't have to let out much rode to get the proper scope on our plow. Lots of cleanup work to do below and then hopefully allow some relax time in the cockpit. I wanted to do a quick check of the hull first to see if any damage might have resulted from either of our contacts with the bottom of the ocean. Scuba mask, snorkel, and lifeline, and over the side I went. First, I want to check how well the has anchor set, it looks like we were hooked fast to the bottom. Next, I inspected the rudder, prop, and keel for any damage. Everything appears to be in good shape. NICE! I wish I could take the time to enjoy the array of tropical life happening just below the surface. Damn, my first dive, it had to be in a hurry, and can not take the time to enjoy.

Back aboard the comfort of our boat, it is time to break out the Wild Turkey 101. No foo foo glass of wine for this skipper this time. Kathy has her usual wine and is still looking very stressed. There seems to be some tension during our usually pleasant end of day chat. Huh...I wonder why?

Note to log; I really need to figure out an easier boarding system...that stern boarding ladder is difficult even in good conditions.

This has proven to be an awful time to have quit smoking.

Over the VHF radio, we get a surprising call;

"Pepper V calling *Walkabout.*"

"Go ahead Pepper V, This is *Walkabout.*"

"Welcome. Fun getting in here huh? Nice show you guys put on. Do you happen to be friends with the crew of Wavedancer?"

"Yes! We were sailing with them."

"They warned us...awe, make that asked us, to keep a watch out for you. They sheltered here for a couple of days then left yesterday for Nassau. They asked us to tell you they will wait in Nassau for your arrival."

"So they only went a few miles further after leaving us off of Grand Bahama," I said to Kathy. She did manage a small grin at that.

"Thank you, Pepper V. It's exciting to hear from them."

It is very cool to run into another boater somewhere in the islands and get a message from another boat that they met a few days earlier. How cool is that? Just like Dieter said.

Unfortunately, the wind is starting to build, and we need to think about our anchor watch. "We will need to keep watch all night long in four-hour shifts to make sure we aren't dragging. With the number of other boats on the hook, it's kind of tight here."

Kathy is just totally exhausted, so I am going to take the first watch while she tries to catch some sleep. The wind started shifting later during the night, so I started the Perkins as a precaution. This wakes up Kathy of course. The 20-25 knot wind has continued its shift coming from the west toward the east, and now our stern is looking at some ugly looking rocks, and we are dangerously close to them.

The idea behind starting the Perkins is to have an immediate backup plan in the event my anchor started to lose its hold...I can just put it in gear to relieve the strain.

"Out of sight of land the sailor feels safe. It is the beach that worries him." -Charles C. Davis

We started out being on the lee side of the island, and we are now on the windward side. I have depleted my inventory of dramatic cuss-word rants at this point. My cursing God hasn't helped our predicament and seems to have only made things worse. Go figure! I thought we were friends.

Kathy is awake for good now but can't/won't man the cockpit by herself, so I guess I'm gonna pull an all-niter. I really don't blame her.

"We may have to reset our anchor to keep us off the rocks. I don't want to set a second anchor right now in case the wind shifts again. That is always an option if it gets any worse. We can also use the engine to dodge any of the other boats that may drift our way." This statement didn't seem to make her feel any better.

In my own sick way, I'm enjoying the challenge of all this. I'm also sure that I can't say the same for my first mate. I am losing command of my ship and respect from the crew damn it! I feel so bad for her but proud that she is hanging in here. These new developments are keeping my mind off of thinking about the near disaster getting in here yesterday. Sure not dull so far!

Things have gotten better this morning, so we are able to relax a little bit, take a break, and think about our next move from here.

"How are you feeling, I'm worried about you," I asked with loving concern. "This is not as fun as we had imagined it would be is it?" my dream had become our dream, and so far it's not been all that much fun. "I need to know your true feelings about which way to head from here, Kathy."

Her face is showing the concern that she is wrestling with, but with the sly grin of the adventurous person that she is..."I think we should push on at least to Nassau."

I was so relieved to hear her say that. We both hate defeat, and we still want to realize the thrill of this fantasy adventure.

"There is supposed to be a decent weather window for the next few days, would you like to try for Little Harbour and anchor there for the night?" I asked.

"Here, read about it, looks fairly easy." handing her the guide book. "We should be able to do it in about four hours."

Her smile is almost returning...I think. We're growing stronger with this sailing stuff. The reasons for my admiration of sailors are becoming clear. This applies to all ocean-going boaters, power and sail! They are a very hearty and adaptable group. We really want to be like them.

THE RUN FOR LITTLE HARBOR
32

Jan. 24 we raised anchor and departed Panton Cove around 9:30 am under partly cloudy sky's, an 8 mph breeze, and calm seas with *Crawlabout* in tow. *Walkabout* is a happy boat again. All is well this morning, and we are excited about restarting our sail to Nassau. We have renewed confidence that it will get better. "Steer 140° toward 25° 33' 30 N 077° 42' 30 W."

Finally, this is the kind of sailing we were looking forward to. With the breeze at our back and the calm sea, we had a nice sail and could relax for the most part. Kathy managed to get in a little reading and take a nap while I am busy soaking up the thrill of the salt air and quiet swoosh *Walkabout* sang when slicing thru the gentle swells. I am in the 'zone' at the helm.

Access into Little Barbour is pretty straight forward with our shoal draft. Much of the anchorage has barely four feet of water at slack tide, so we need to anchor with swing room in mind just in case. There are also some strong tidal currents with barely enough room for two boats. Fortunately, there is only one other boat anchored, Don and June, a Canadian couple aboard Pepper V. We met them at Great Stirrup and they were the ones that gave us the message from Wavedancer.

We anchored between Little Harbour Cay and Cabbage Cay.

Once we settled in, I took Crawlabout out to check how our had anchor set in the sand bottom using the glass bottom bucket I had made. This is such a handy tool to have aboard.

If there is any truth to the old saying "we learn from our mistakes" then we will be the smartest crew to ever have a deck under their feet...if we live that long. It seems that while I wasn't paying attention, Crawlabout had set itself free to explore the area and ride the current out toward the sea. Pepper V came to our rescue by retrieving the runaway tender. With the way things have gone, I would hate to think about not having our little life raft that provided some sense of security in case of a disaster.

We invited the Pepper V crew to join us for cocktails later so we could hear about their adventures and properly thank them for all their help.

Last night we enjoyed a comfortable, well deserved, beautiful nights sleep in our ideal little anchorage. Shortly after sunrise, while having coffee in the cockpit, I watched Pepper V weigh anchor to head out for the next part of their voyage.

"*Walkabout* to Pepper V, have a good trip and thank you again for all your help. We hope to see you again."

"*Walkabout*...Pepper V, you're very welcome and good luck to you. Say hello to Wavedancer when you see them," came their reply.

And so I watched them leave the island in admiration of the adventures they have had and are heading off for.

Kathy finally came up to the cockpit, looking rested, sexy, and more like her happy self..."Good morning sweetheart. Who are you talking to?"

I pointed to Pepper V as they were hoisting her sail while heading out of the anchorage toward the sea. With her sails full, and the power of the wind taking over the energy of propulsion, she sailed off into the sunrise. "I'll get you a cup of coffee, and then we can plan our day. Such a glorious morning it is!"

We decided to spend our day anchored in this charming cove to enjoy new found peace and the real joy of this island anchoring life. We packed a lunch and took a welcome shore leave on Crawlabout around a point to a secluded beach we passed on our way into the anchorage. We are going to do a little island exploring and build a sandcastle or two...kid stuff kind of stuff.

Climbing a small hill gave us a perfect view of our slice of heaven anchorage. I couldn't pass up this photo op. Finally, after many thousands of $$$$$ and years of planning, "WE DID IT!" this is the realization of the thrill we had imagined. The way we knew it could be.

"I never really appreciated the refreshing value of a nap until I swung in a hammock while lying at anchor in a quiet bay......" A Long

As we are hiking up a hill, we took time to enjoy a postcard-perfect shot of *Walkabout* lying peacefully at anchor.

"What do you think Kathy, is this worth the effort that it's taken to get here,? I asked.

"It sure comes close skipper, I love it," came her reply.

We continued our climb to the top of the hill and explored an old house that looks as if it had been, at one time, fabulous back in its day.

The realization of what was once "just an imaginable day" is pleasurably fulfilling.

Back aboard *Walkabout,* Kathy wanted to pleasure herself with a nap while I am taking the time to update our log and review the last 24 hours in my mind and on paper. I want to relive those moments just for the sheer joy of it.

Kathy gets in a little reading while I figure our course to Nassau. It's time to update our little computer system. I love it! I keep a printout of the inventory at the nav station, so it is easy to look-up and locate any item that's needed. When an item is taken, it is marked on the sheets and can be updated and sorted in the computer to print out an up-to-date shopping list when we reach Nassau.

Settling in for the evening with a light meal, along with our glass of wine, we take the time to enjoy each others company and soak it all in.

Our day and evening are a perfect match to the way we imagined this lifestyle would be like. While sitting in the cockpit and enjoying a beautiful sunset with our wine and some low island music provided by Jimmy Buffet, we made our plans to head on to Nassau in the morning. "I figure we can make it in about seven hours with the forecast winds," I say.

Ships log: Our cockpit times remind me of all the evenings we would spend at my house on a deck overlooking the horse pasture. Listening to them graze and an occasional "sneezing" sound the horses make. The dogs lying in the grass chewing on their bones and my precious cat Maggie out with the horses. We would talk and laugh about everything, and make plans to go sailing one day.

There is an explosion of the universe quietly happening in the sky above us. Totally glorious ceiling made of stars, and rivals the nighttime sky view in the remote Colorado mountains. The bay is calm with a slightly moving reflection of the stars above. There are no unnatural lights anywhere to interfere with nature...it's like being on a distant planet. The hunter Orion silently passes overhead during the night. I had gotten into a habit of looking for him years ago...he gives me comfort.

I can now see the tan-line of Kathy's bikini showing on her naked body...it almost appears she is still wearing it. This is turning into one of those special romantic evenings that a lot of us guys think about...a lot!

I am very relieved that there are no other boats around to hear our expressions of joy with each other tonight. An explosive evening all around.

NASSAU AT LAST
33

1-26-'92;

Up at 5:00 am and making coffee while I double check our course plans, and listen to the weather forecast. I am on my second cup of brew when Kathy appears in the cockpit after smelling the alluring fresh brew. She is sporting a glow.

"How about I make us some bacon and eggs for breakfast?" she asked. "We'll need to have a good meal under our belts for the trip," she added.

"That would be perfect, I just hope it stays under our belt," I jokingly replied.

As Kathy cleaned up after breakfast and stowed things below-deck, I double checked all deck lashings paying special attention to our inflatable. We opted to bring Crawlabout back aboard on the fore-deck.

Sunday; 7:50 am our anchor is up and we are heading out of Little Harbour Cay by steering 140° under mostly cloudy skies. We have a light to moderate breeze from the east at about 10 knots. We are sailing close-hauled under a full main and genoa while cutting thru the waves at about 6 knots. "I feel the power," I inform Kathy, "I am the king of the world."

"Don't let it go to your head commander," she blurted out, along with some other words that seemed not so kind.

"Speaking of head...I saved your ass the other day remember?" I'm thinking maybe I could've worded that a little better. I received no reply...not even "the look."

About an hour into our sail, the wind has picked up to 12-14 knots. The sky is starting to clear nicely as we made a course correction to 150°. Matt-auto-helm is working great...can't say that for loran, however.

This gave me an excellent opportunity to practice my dead-reckoning skills again. Many large ships allowed me to check our position with them over the radio and compare to my "reckon." Some of those ships weren't even trying to run us down. I enjoy going below to chart our position about every 30 minutes...I am getting pretty good at this. I take pleasure working at my little nav-station. The nav-station is a short trip from the wheel and is fairly tight quarters. Nice fit in rough seas. The radar is working hard to give me the critical information I need about the course and speed of other ships. Kathy is keeping an eye on the auto-helm, compass, and acting as lookout.

I can get lost here...it's like being in another world, hiding behind my charts, course plotter, my dividers, and parallel rules, and only my fellow pirates can see me.

Later this morning, around 11:00, the wind has increased to close to 20 knots with some stronger gusts. We have improved our sea legs and our sailing skills over the last several days, and have gotten used to some of the thrashing about and what to expect.

I took over the steering of the boat, with Kathy sitting beside me, reading.

I'm really enjoying this ride and falling more in love with this lady. But, I wonder...

Since this sail is more controlled and relaxed than the last several days, I want to take some time and see if I can detect how Kathy is really feeling about this adventure so far. I keep getting mixed messages and am not positive how she actually feels. Sometimes it seems like a mutiny may be brewing. I see some changes in her behavior at times. More *uneasy* than easy.

Around noon land was sighted..."Land Ho!" It's so exciting to finally make it to New Providence and Paradise Islands. The city of Nassau is located on New Providence and is the capital of the Bahamas. Besides just the thrilling experience of the trip, I, we, are looking forward to seeing this legendary city. We want to enjoy the city and its people. Alluring Paradise Island is just across the bridge.

2:45 pm we saw the white tower on Silver Cay first and then the lighthouse on the western tip of Paradise Island. We just need to aim between the two and stay closer to the buoy and lighthouse on our port side to enter the channel.

"Wavedancer, Wavedancer, Walkabout, over," Kathy couldn't stand to wait any longer. Repeat.

"Walkabout, Walkabout, Wavedancer, 68, over," came back a reply that put an instant smile on the crews face. "copy 68."

Wavedancer; "Walkabout, welcome to Nassau... we knew you could do it! We'll give you directions to the docks at Nassau Yacht Haven where we'll be waiting."

After passing under the Paradise Island Bridge, we can see the large marina on our starboard and then simply followed Dieter's directions to our slip. BY GOD...THERE THEY ARE!

It's a picture-perfect docking!

Kathy has already deployed our dock bumpers, readied the boat-hook, and attached the spring-lines. It' gratifying to see all the practice in action. We welcome their help getting us in and making us somewhat secure for the moment. We couldn't wait to hit the dock and hug our friends. But first, I planted a big kiss on the wood decking of the pier...then, hugs to both.

We are here, really here, and still can't believe it is actually being realized. We invited Dieter and Rosemary to come aboard for a beer while Kathy and I finish our docking routine of making sure everything is secure, and that unneeded gear is properly stowed. "Don't forget to plug in the shore power," I was told. "We need to have a fan running to air things out, and make it cooler for this evening."

Dieter filled us in on their plans for heading on down to Allen's Cay in the Northern Exuma chain, about 35 miles, on the morning of the 28th and want us to go with them.

"That doesn't leave much time for sightseeing or relaxing," Kathy said, "and we need to do some shopping...we need a new anchor for one thing," she said with a smirk. "We'll tell you all about that tonight."

Both Dieter and Rosemary agreed that we would not miss much by not seeing Nassau. Not very tourist friendly, except down by the cruise ship docks, and that's a mess. Lots of pickpockets like almost any other city.

"We have dinner reservations at the Poop Deck for the four crew-members," Rosemary said with a smile, "Our treat...we wanna hear all the details about your trip."

While we are getting ready to go to dinner, we

decided we would push on and go with Wavedancer. I am still getting an uneasy feeling that things aren't right with the happiness of the crew, but we need to press on. We are still pumped-up about eventually finding sandy beaches to play on and coral reefs to dive.

With only one day to get ready, we will have to go shopping for the new anchor and other stuff, as well as our food store replacements.

I'll make a computer list of the stuff we need," I said with a grin.

THE QUEST FOR ALLEN'S CAY
34

Early morning Jan 28;

I am taking advantage of this early (3 am) quiet time to update the ship's log:

> *"Casting off early this morning. We have accomplished so much during the past month. I am amazed and proud we finally made it this far. Kathy and I have become quite a crew at handling some very frightening situations. So far, this trip has been intense and unnerving instead of the romantic cruise we had envisioned. Walkabout has performed beyond my expectations, with the exception of the injector tube fiasco. Solid boat, I am happy with my choice. I am still a little uneasy about the future and what might lay ahead, but this is one of the unknown things that make this adventure so thrilling. The crew is hanging in there so far. We are heading out early this morning and ready for the next challenge with a lot of island hopping."*

My wishlist is growing already. 1. A small 110 V generator. I never want not to have a way to charge my batteries. 2.

A GPS, but need to wait for prices to come down. 3. Some type of better boarding ladder or prefer a swim platform. 4. Better VCR and music tape storage. 5. Larger outboard for Crawlabout.

My first mate is waking up and needs coffee.

At the eastern end of Athol Island near Porgee Rocks, we alter course to take advantage of deeper water, for *Wavedancer's* benefit, using a dog-leg route to Allen's Cay in the Exuma Islands.

With the weather forecast calling for 25-28 knot winds from the east and rain squalls..."Hoist the main and put a reef in it," I bravely shouted to the crew. "Off we go again mate!".........

So far this has been an excitingly unimaginable trip in every way. Unimaginable meaning...who would have thought. Some ways good and some not so good, but with a combination of hard-learned skill and lots of luck we have made it this far. A big regret is that we couldn't take the time to explore and enjoy the few islands we had already visited. God still hasn't forgiven me for that outburst back at Great Stirrup Cay, I think. Or...was it the boat name change??

The reality is we are doing this instead of being at home mowing the grass. (I do love lying in the freshly mowed grass, however.)

To be continued in A SAIL ABOARD WALKABOUT-Book B. Due out early next year.

*The events in **Ships log-Book A** took place in the first 10 months of buying Walkabout. There are so many other events, some pleasurable and some not so pleasurable, that happened over the next four years, that I felt the need to end this chapter of the log after achieving this first major goal...reaching Nassau.*

I owned Walkabout for almost four more years, and I have many more stories to share...just couldn't do it all in one book. Besides, I really need the money.

Every event that I've written about actually happened. I've tried to reflect each individual's personality as close as possible...the way I saw them, anyway.

At the very least, after reading this, I hope you have gotten some enjoyment, gained some knowledge, and given you some encouragement to challenge yourself to pursue your own dreams.

I simply wanted to see if I (we) could do it!

Alan

SHIPS LOG-BOOK B CONTINUE THE SAIL ABOARD WALKABOUT
35

A peek at what's to come!

Surprise!!! More storms, beautiful beaches, numerous sharks, exotic islands, and a lot of wonderfully interesting sailors await us.

The inevitable mutiny by the crew (I know you see that coming) is not a lot of fun. What kind of sail adventure would it be without a hurricane or two? Andrew in Key Largo, and then the no-name hurricane in Boot Key Harbor.

How about being lost at sea while diving and then making the evening news? Peter and the pig, Howie and the "bitter end," beach party's, nude walks on the beach, and romantic dinners. A very inspiring Christmas with the rangers at Fort Jefferson in the Tortugas with a touching gift exchange, by candlelight, a battery-powered tape deck with the Christmas music echoing off the brick walls of the fort,...fantastic!

Bless this boat and its crew...

ABOUT THE AUTHOR
36

I had the very fortunate blessing to grow up in a small mid-west town under the direction of some loving parents and wonderful brothers. I can't thank them enough. I wish **every** child could have that opportunity.

In the 50s I was a "leave it to Beaver" kind of boy. I never fit into any particular group, so I tried them all to no avail. Tried being a "punk" but found out I wasn't good at it, and I certainly wasn't a jock, I wore dark frame glasses that were held together with tape on the nose for gosh sake. We moved to a truly "colorful Colorado" in the fabulous 60s with real-life American Graffiti kind of stuff, just like in the movies...chasing girls, cruising, drag racing, and chocolate malts. A terrific family and a new group of friends, a very rewarding time.

In the mid-60s I bought a cabin in the mountains. It was my place of solitude for my reality checks. Still not fitting in, but was enjoying the ride. A brutal reality check was when my older brother was killed by a drunk driver when he was just 23. My outlook on life changed at that point, I needed to enjoy every single day. I needed to take my unhinged personality and turn it into something positive.

Skiing, flying, drag racing, golf, fireman, cowboy, sailor, entrepreneur, husband, and father...always looking for a vacant cog that I could fill.

Part-time college, then a successful IBM salesman to finish out the 60s and 70s. The 70s also saw me get married to the woman of my dreams that gave us the most precious daughter any parents could wish for.

In 1980 I started my business just in time for the woman of my dreams to divorce me. Tough time during tough times. Thankfully, the business became a success. I continued to miss my family, so I bought a boat......

52813777R00136

Made in the USA
Lexington, KY
20 September 2019